© 2021 Gary Keltner
All Rights Reserved

Except by a reviewer who may quote brief passages in a review, without written permission of the author no part of this book may be reproduced in any form or by any method, including by any electronic, mechanical or other means.

Although reasonable efforts have been made to assure the material accuracy and completeness of the information contained in this book, no assurance can be given that there are no errors, inaccuracies, inconsistencies or omissions. Any slights or misstatements are unintended.

ISBN: 978-0-578-93262-0
Library of Congress Control Number: 2021912428

Printed in the United States of America.

First General Publication Edition
Self-published

Table of Contents

Special Thanks	v
Dedication	vi
Author's Preface	vii
A Perspective: The "Hoosiers" and the "Vandals"	x
Introduction	xii
PROLOGUE	1
The Globe-Miami Area	12
The Town of Miami	14
Nearby Globe	18
The 1950-51 Miami Vandals	38
Coach Kivisto	39
Miami's Team	44
The Regular Season	46

Week One
    Friday, December 8, 1950: Miami (win); Fort Thomas (forfeit)
    Saturday, December 9, 1950: Miami 78; St. Johns 41
	48

Week Two
    Friday, December 15, 1950: Miami 63; Superior 41
    Saturday, December 16, 1950: Miami 87; Thatcher 39
	53

Week Three
    Thursday, December 21, 1950: Miami 74; Bisbee 35
    Friday, December 22, 1950: Miami 56; Nogales 50
	55

Week Four
    Thursday, December 28, 1950: Miami 101; Flagstaff 28
    Friday, December 29, 1950: Miami 79; Winslow 32
	57

Week Five
    Friday, January 5, 1951: Miami 94; Duncan 38
    Saturday, January 6, 1951: Miami 94; Safford 50
	59

Week Six Friday, January 12, 1951: Miami 122; Clifton 58 Saturday, January 13, 1951: Miami 56; Pima 28	61
Week Seven Friday, January 19, 1951: Miami 80; Pima 21 Saturday, January 20, 1951: Miami (win); Fort Thomas (forfeit)	64
Week Eight Thursday, January 25, 1951: Miami 77; Morenci 44 Friday, January 26, 1951: Miami 92; Clifton 72 Saturday, January 27, 1951: Miami 99; Duncan 47	64
Week Nine Friday, February 2, 1951: Miami 57; Thatcher 39 Saturday, February 3, 1951: Miami 72; Safford 43	66
Week Ten Friday, February 9, 1951: Miami 130; Morenci 43	68
Week Eleven Friday, February 16, 1951: Miami 105; Globe 61 Saturday, February 17, 1951: Miami 102; Globe 49	72
Regular Season Recap	76
The Eastern Conference Tournament	79
Week Twelve (in Globe) Thursday, February 22, 1951): Miami 88; Safford 30 Friday, February 23, 1951: Miami 95; Globe 49 Saturday, February 24, 1951: Miami 57; Pima 42	81
Conference Tournament Recap	84
The State Tournament	85
Week Thirteen (in Tucson) Thursday, March 1, 1951: Miami 96; Holbrook 70 Friday, March 2, 1951: Miami 104; Scottsdale 51 Saturday, March 3, 1951: Miami 72; Clifton 58 Saturday, March 3, 1951: Miami 58; Phoenix Carver 50	90

State Tournament Recap	98
Season Recap	99
Post-Season	100
Closing Perspective	105
The Vandals' Legacy	107
EPILOGUE	108
Appendix 1: More About Coach Kivisto and His Family	110
Appendix 2: Miami's Players	122
Lupe Acevedo	122
Elias Delgadillo (Huerta)	124
Hector Jacott	125
Leigh Larson	126
Eli ("Ted" / "Teddy") Lazovich	128
Alfred ("Al") Lobato	130
Rudy ("Pelon") Moreno	131
Andrew ("Andy") Rumic	132
Adolpho ("Fito") Trujillo	133
Dick ("Dickie") Vargas	135
Jesus Romero, Manager	136
Nick Ragus	137
Cheerleaders	138
Twirlers	139
Dating at Last	140
Appendix 3: Miami Practice Drills	141
Appendix 4: Coach Kivisto's Post-Season Handout to Players	142
Appendix 5: Miami Players at Arizona State College - Flagstaff	148
Appendix 6: Dr. Marin's Social Commentary	152
Appendix 7: Miami Opponents	162
George Washington Carver High School	162
Hadie Redd (Phoenix Carver)	163
Charles Christopher (Phoenix Carver)	164
Porfirio "Buddy" Islas (Nogales)	165
Morenci High School	165
Appendix 8: Globe High Profiles	167

Max Spilsbury	167
John Pavlich	180
Ken Troutt	184
Ed Nymeyer	185
Appendix 9: Selected Writings, Movies and Media Involving Globe-Miami, Gila County and Nearby Superior	189

Appendix 10: Arizona Maps
    Arizona Interstate and U.S. Highways
    Portion of Arizona with Teams Miami Defeated
	192

About the Author	194

The Vandals' Yearbook

Special Thanks

Alphabetically, those who helped the author ascertain and verify facts for this chronicle include:

"Dickie" Dicus
Tom Henry
Bob Kivisto
Dr. Christine Marin
Miami High School
Edwin "Pudge" Nymeyer
John Pavlich
Paul Pavlich
Wilfred "Sonny" Gomez Pena
Mary (Pavlich) Roby
Andy Rumic
Joaquin "Juke" Sanchez
Teddy Sorich
Max Spilsbury family members
"Fito" Trujillo
John Trujillo
Radovan Lolly ("Rad") Vucichevich

Special thanks to Gary Stuart, a long-time friend and fellow law partner at Jennings Strouss (established in 1942), and the author of several books, for his insights regarding publication and printing. There have been others, too. I appreciate and thank them for their contributions.

Dedication

We are products of those who have touched us profoundly. This chronicle is dedicated to two of those who touched me most.

Max Spilsbury, my first high school football and junior varsity basketball coach, found in me and helped unleash a fierce competitive fire. He rewarded my efforts with bursts of joy and affirmation, and once told me, "With your attitude, you can do anything you ever want to do." To a shy sophomore, from a Marine Ranger whom I intensely respected and admired, those words instilled confidence and have immeasurably impacted my life.

John Pavlich, his successor as my varsity football and basketball coach, was a humorous, kind and thoughtful man who, contrary to Leo Durocher's legendary proclamation, proved by example that nice guys do not finish last. A veteran of the Pacific War and a friend until his death, he, too, importantly impacted my life then and since.[1]

---

[1] The author was also privileged to play for another excellent coach and exemplary person, **Ken Troutt**, who assisted Coaches Spilsbury and Pavlich. *Appendix 8* includes biographical information about Coaches Spilsbury, Pavlich and Troutt.

Author's Preface

This is the story of a group of small-town young men and their coach of immigrant-American heritages (Mexican, Slavic and Scandinavian) who, soon after WWII and in the deepening shadow of a new war in Korea, lit up the Arizona basketball world and gained national attention.

Six decades later, writing for the Globe-Miami Times in October 2010, Linda Gross wrote of the 1950-51 Vandals:

> There are storied moments in history which shine light on those who made history and those who remember it long past the actual event. The Dream Team of 1951 made up of mostly Mexican kids from Bullion Plaza led by Vandals Coach Ernie Kivisto created many magic moments during that season which still resonate nearly 60 years later with the re-telling.

Envisioned for years as a carefully written book, and thus delayed because of difficulties ascertaining and confirming a relatively few small and largely unimportant details, this has been the mother of all procrastinations. Only because I became reconciled to it becoming instead a largely informative chronicle has it come to fruition.

Beginning in high school, I collected information and for decades wrote partial drafts. But I delayed because I wanted to do the story justice and -- with a busy law practice, marriage, family and the vagaries of life – distractions and time were issues. Time remains an issue, but now because the time to finish has grown short. Most of those involved have died; and more will soon slip away.

Presented with a choice of having this published professionally or, while still alive simply making its content available for the information it contains without professional guidance, formatting and other frills, I have chosen the latter, without jumping through time-consuming hoops required of the former. Thus, instead of the literate, carefully crafted book I once envisioned, this is a reportorial compilation based on my own observations and research, and supplemented by anecdotal input from some participants, family members, observers and other sources. I hope it will inform new generations, and remind older ones, of what Miami's young boys and their coach accomplished for themselves, the town, and the area; and that it will remind those of us who grew up in Miami and Globe during that period how fortunate we were to have done so.

As a Globe High School freshman, I watched the 1950-51 Miami Vandals play several games -- in Miami, in Globe and at the Eastern Conference tournament. Their grace, speed, efficiency and talent were and have remained imbedded in my psyche. To this day, in my mind's eye, I see the white and green satin uniformed Vandals flying down the court the night they scored a national record 130 points against Morenci -- with the ball seeming only rarely to hit the floor and many passes point blank beneath the basket.

The need to simply get this done has led to acceptance of some relatively immaterial anecdotal information at face value, without independent verification. However, based on my own recollections, knowledge and research, much of it decades ago, I am comfortable that the matters reported are essentially correct.[2] There can be no doubt that the accomplishments of the 1950-51 basketball Vandals and their coach merit the revived and perhaps more permanent recognition this chronicle may help provide them.

Beyond that, sprinkled with some personal anecdotes, this chronicle provides a brief mid-20th Century glimpse of two ethnically mixed Arizona mining towns – Miami and Globe – just a few years after World War II. For context and perspective, it includes a potpourri of

---

[2] Except as noted, quoted material has been presented as written, including some relatively unimportant inconsistencies, mistakes and clerical issues.

peripheral information. I have referenced some history and contemporary events and attitudes -- political, international, social, and sports. I also have noted college and other high school game scores to illustrate the dramatically lower scoring environment that existed in 1950-51. I have added information about teams, players and coaches whose paths intersected that of the Vandals during their remarkable season. And I have tried to provide a sense of the twin communities in which I feel so fortunate to have grown up.

One more thing. Except for those here when the Europeans arrived, we are all descended of immigrants. Without being judgmental and while trying to be reasonably sensitive, I am not a fan of political correctness. To me, it is an enemy of honest expression – a tacit form of censorship. And it is confusing. Unknowably to a writer, it exists differently in the minds of each beholder and can change overnight. It can ban writings of Hemmingway and Mark Twain (as it sometimes has) or condemn them to lock boxes from which they can be removed and read only on request. Bret Harte's "Heathen Chinee" -- Was that pejorative or disrespectful? If so, to whom – the wily Chinese immigrant who conned his fellow Euchre players in the game "he did not understand" or the two who were "had" by him? And, like much satire, didn't it challenge the stereotype? When in 1962 Martin Luther King made his acclaimed "I have a dream" speech at the Lincoln Memorial he repeatedly described his race as "the Negro," but now the common usage is "African-American" or simply "Blacks" or "blacks." Bottom line, I no longer know what is and is not politically correct terminology. If some of my thoughts and observations are expressed in words considered by a reader as inappropriate, please consider that they are well-intended, non-judgmental, and imply no disrespect.

A Perspective: The "Hoosiers" and the Vandals

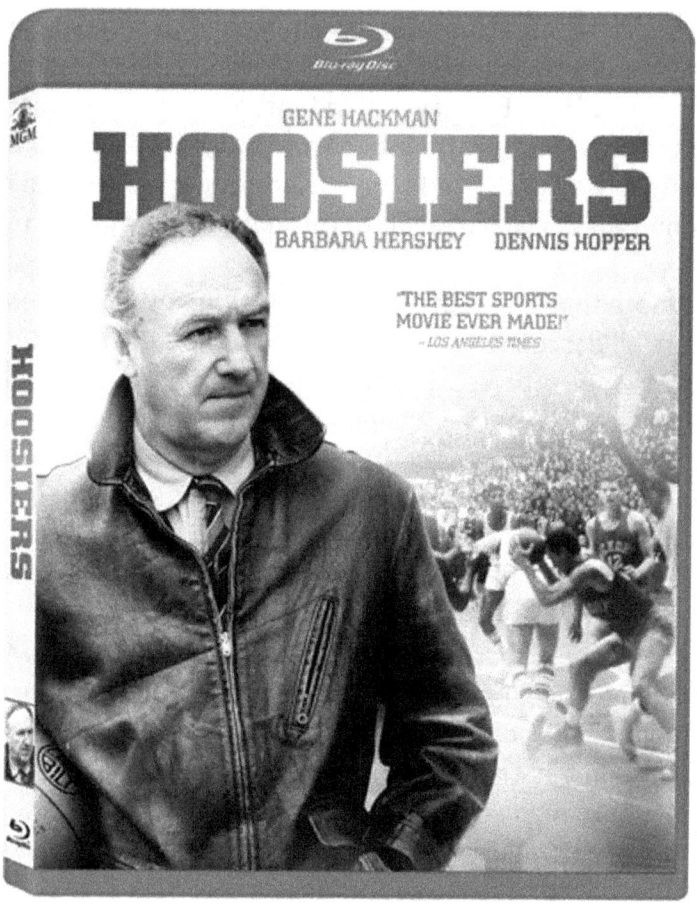

In 1954, Milan Indiana's Indians defeated Muncie Central's Bearcats 32-30 to win the unified Indiana state basketball championship. Milan was a town of about 2,000 with a high school enrollment of about 160. Muncie Central was a big city school with a large enrollment. Milan's improbable victory became the basis of "The Hoosiers" – the 1986 cult classic for which Gene Hackman, as the small-town coach, was nominated for an Academy Award.

In 1951, three years before Milan's celebrated feat, the Miami Arizona Vandals defeated Phoenix Carver's Monarchs 58-50 to win

Arizona's state Class B basketball championship.[3] Like Milan, Miami was a town of a few thousand, with a small high school enrollment. Pre-desegregation, Carver was Phoenix's all African American high school and a perennial basketball powerhouse.

The Vandals' victory crowned one of the most remarkable seasons in the history of high school basketball. En route to their championship, the Vandals were undefeated, set a national high school single-game scoring record, and during a four-week period had three different players break Arizona's single-game scoring mark.

Perhaps it is time for another movie -- this time about a small, ethnically diverse, Arizona mining town at mid-20th Century and about the pride instilled by a few hard-working, well-coached young men whose accomplishments exceeded any that had come before. The story of its passionate, innovative coach and his immigrant family could itself be the basis for a story about the heights to which a family beginning with virtually nothing can rise. That, however, is a story to be written by others. Hopefully, it will be.

---

[3] Except for a few schools with small enrollments, in the early 1950s Arizona's high school athletic programs were either Class A or Class B. The Class A schools -- with the largest enrollments -- were all in Phoenix, plus Tucson High School and Yuma High School. The Class B schools included some Phoenix schools, the other Tucson schools, and the rest of Arizona. The Class B schools were organized into five conferences, with Miami in the Eastern. Each conference held its own tournament to determine its representatives at the State Tournament.

Introduction

By Ed Nymeyer[4]

Because I was often playing elsewhere on the freshman team of their rival Globe Tigers, I saw the 1950-51 Miami Vandals play only a few times. But those games left a lasting impression. Miami was coached by Ernie Kivisto and he molded his young boys into a great basketball team.

In those days, neighboring teams often played back-to-back games on Friday and Saturday nights. The games were big events in our small towns of Globe and Miami. There was standing room only for most games. If I had not been playing on Globe's freshman team, which played the preliminary game against Miami's freshman team, I might not have gotten into the gym for Globe-Miami's two season-ending rivalry games. Once inside, I watched the varsity games from the top level of the bleachers.

In 1951, Globe played the first of the back-to-back games on Miami's home court. I don't remember the score of my freshman game that night, but I'll never forget the varsity score -- Miami 105; Globe 61! And our guys weren't that bad!

The Vandals were not just an exceptional team. They had class, too; and they made quite an entrance. At halftime of the junior varsity games preceding the varsity games, the entire Miami team would enter the gym dressed in *suits and ties*. As they paraded in, their fans went wild with shouts and cheers. It was intimidating.

---

[4] "Pudge," as he was often called (although he wasn't overweight), is a basketball member of the University of Arizona Sports Hall of Fame and, for boys' basketball and girls' volleyball, a member of the Arizona Interscholastic Coaches' Hall of Fame. Biographical information is in *Appendix 8*.

In the first game against Globe, the Vandals pressed from the start, destroying the Tigers during the first three minutes. Things went downhill from there. The Miami crowd loved it. Their style of play overcame every team in the conference, so we weren't alone in our futility.

The next night on our home court in Globe was worse. We "held" the Vandals to just 102 points but managed to score only 49. Frustrating!

In those days, for a high school team -- or even a college or professional team -- to score a hundred points in a game was rare. Even today, it is a feat few high school teams achieve. There was no shot clock. There were no three-point shots. I shudder to think what Miami's scores would have been if the three-point shot had existed then. There was no dunking. If a player even touched the rim, it was a violation. Every basket came from actually making a shot. In addition, opponents could choose to take the ball out of bounds when fouled rather than shoot free throws. That permitted them to maintain possession, stall if they chose, and try to keep the score down.

I coached high school basketball for more than 30 years and was successful -- having been inducted as a coach into the Pima County Sports Hall of Fame and the Arizona Coach's Hall of Fame. Yet, I had only one game in which my boys scored over 100 points. I tried to copy Coach Kivisto's style of play, and his Vandals' full-court press and fast break, but I never achieved it, even though I had some excellent players and state championship teams.

I consider the 1950-51 Vandals the best "team" in the history of Arizona high school basketball. Other teams have had better overall talent (some of mine did), but I never saw a group of boys play better together.

They made a lasting impression on me. After 70 years I still recall the names of their starting five: Lupe Acevedo, Fito Trujillo, Eli Lazovich, Rudy Moreno, and Hector Jacott. For perspective, I don't remember the names of all the guys who started with me that year on Globe's freshman team, or who started on our varsity team.

Several of the 1950-51 Vandals went on to play college basketball. I didn't track them all, but I'd bet that each would say the 1950-51 basketball season was the most memorable and enjoyable sports year of his life. As an athlete and coach, I know how special it is to be part of a great team. I would have liked to have been part of that team.

PROLOGUE

In late 1950, five miles west of Globe, Arizona, above the low, chaparral-covered hills between Globe and Miami, the cold, dark, December night sky began to glow. Slowly at first, it turned faint orange, then brightened and turned red. At Inspiration Consolidated Copper Company, molten slag was being dumped from rail cars down a black lava hillside. Its glow lit the sky. In Miami, a mile further west, another glow was about to light the western sky.

Arizona was then just 38 years from statehood. Less than 30 years before that, the shootout at the OK Corral, the final surrender of Geronimo and his small band of Apaches, and the deadly Pleasant Valley War with its undetermined body count of more than 30 had occurred. The years between were highlighted by World War I, World War II and, on the lurid crime front, Phoenix's infamous "Trunk Murderess."[5]

The Pleasant Valley War

---

[5] In what Life Magazine termed one of the most sensational crimes of the first half of the 20th Century, 26-year-old Winnie Ruth Judd, dubbed by some the "Tiger Lady," shipped the dismembered bodies of two roommates by rail to Los Angeles where they were discovered in two trunks on the unloading dock. For an account, see Jana Bommersbach's *The Trunk Murderess: Winnie Ruth Judd* (NY, Simon & Shuster 1992).

> The Pleasant Valley War has been the subject of numerous books, historical and fictional, including *Arizona's Dark and Bloody Ground* by Earle Forrest, Don Dedera's *A Little War of Our Own* and Zane Grey's *To the Last Man*. The dust cover of the latter states:
>
>> There really was a terrible and bloody feud, perhaps the most deadly and least known in all the annals of the West. I saw the ground, the cabins, the graves, all so darkly suggestive of what must have happened.
>
> More recently, Jinx Pyle has written what may be the most authoritative account of *The Pleasant Valley War*. The Foreword by Marshall Trimble, Arizona's Official State Historian, states, "[T]he history of the Pleasant Valley War has lived under a shroud of silence. Those who knew the most had the most to lose and, therefore, told the least." With new research and anecdotal family interviews Mr. Pyle has provided new information and insights that have helped pierce the shroud and expose what really happened.

Fueled by the five "Cs" – copper, cattle, citrus, cotton, and climate – Arizona had grown from a wild, dangerous and sparsely settled territory to a state about to burst on the national scene.

In 1950, with the advent of air conditioning and multiple military bases, its two main population centers – Phoenix (then 105,000; now 1.6 million and the 5th most populous city in the United States -- behind New York, Los Angeles, Chicago and Houston) and Tucson (then 45,000; now 546,000), were poised for the major growth that has occurred since.

Fourteen years later, in 1964, Senator Barry Goldwater ("Mr. Conservative") would be the GOP candidate for President. Soon after, John Rhodes would become House Minority Leader for eight years. President Nixon's 1974 resignation would be triggered by a meeting with Senator Goldwater, Congressman Rhodes and Pennsylvania Senator Hugh Scott.[6]

Entered from the east by four major east-west highways, Arizona was the gateway to California and the migrations there during the 30s and 40s. Connecting Chicago and Santa Monica, U.S. 66 (famously, *Route 66*, the *Main Street of America,* or the *Mother Road*) crossed northern Arizona. U.S. 60 ran 2,500 miles from Virginia Beach through Globe and Miami, and on to Los Angeles. U.S. 70 ran from North Carolina to Globe, where it merged with U.S. 60. Connecting Georgia and San Diego, U.S. 80 circuitously crossed the southern part of Arizona through Tucson.

Just five years earlier, in August of 1945, the first atomic bomb had been dropped on Hiroshima, followed by a second on Nagasaki, forcing the Japanese surrender that ended World War II. The war had claimed an estimated 40 to 60 million lives. It would have claimed many more had it continued.

Yet, already, the United States was involved in a "Cold War" with the Soviet Union. And -- across the Pacific Ocean 6,000 miles west of Miami, Arizona – we were involved in a United Nations "police action" to repel North Korea's invasion of South Korea. There, a far more ominous glow was lighting the night sky – the glow of explosions, flares and tracers. Stranded in North Korea and being assaulted at times from just yards away by thousands of Chinese soldiers, U.S. Marine and Army units were trapped in harsh winter near the Chosin Reservoir -- fighting to break out in subzero temperatures, snow and ice. By its end in 1953, the undeclared Korean War would claim more than 54,000 American lives. That war was a foreboding backdrop to Miami's 1950-51 basketball season and would impact the lives of several Miami players.

---

[6] John Rhodes was the father of Scott Rhodes, a partner of the author at, and past Managing Member of, the Jennings Strouss law firm with which the author has been associated since 1964.

Also in October and November of 1950:

- Charles Schultz first published the comic strip *Peanuts*,
- China invaded Tibet,
- The Federal Communications Commission issued the first license to broadcast TV in color,
- In East German elections, the Communists won 97.7 % of the vote,
- Puerto Rican nationalists attempted to assassinate President Harry Truman who was staying at the Blair House near the White House, which was being renovated,
- Flying an F-80, Air Force Lt. Russell Brown intercepted and shot down two North Korean MiG-15s near the Yalu River in history's first jet-to-jet dogfight,
- A U.S. Air Force B-50 Superfortress bomber experienced an in-flight emergency over Quebec, Canada, and jettisoned a nuclear bomb lacking its plutonium core, and
- North America had a population of 171,616,000.

In the weeks before the start of Arizona's 1950-51 high school basketball season, the Arizona Republic (Arizona's largest daily, published in Phoenix) reported:

- the groundbreaking for Miami High School's Memorial Gymnasium to seat 2,700, at a cost of $172,000,
- the closing of school in Payson for fear of polio after a young

boy was sent to Phoenix and placed in an iron lung,

- in French Indochina (including what in 1954 would become Viet Nam) several thousand French troops were pursuing Communist-led native forces while planes bombed and strafed the rebels,

- ten years after the Mexico City assassination of Russian Bolshevik revolutionary leader Leon Trotsky there was still "a veil of mystery around his cryptic killer" with police "unsure of his name, his nationality, or the source of the money which enables him to live in a comfortable suite of cells in the federal penitentiary,"

- having re-read the diary of British General Wolfe (who during the French and Indian War captured Quebec from the French after being told by subordinates that the approach up a twisting footpath to the Plains of Abraham was impossible), General Douglas McArthur, the United Nations commander in Korea, was reported to have been similarly convinced by the "doubts and fears of his subordinates" that what became his daringly successful Inchon landing was a sound strategy,

- in New York, the Yankees and the Phillies "Whiz Kids" were to meet in the first game of the World Series, and Phillies' ace Curt Simmons, whose Pennsylvania National Guard unit had been activated for the Korean conflict, had been granted leave but was not expected to pitch,

- leaving New York for the World Series in Philadelphia, "Whitey Ford, young pitcher who was 21 years old Tuesday, arrived just a minute before train time and got a dozen roses intended for Joe DiMaggio,"

- National League player representative Marty Marion

announced that baseball commissioner A.B. "Happy" Chandler had arranged a meeting "to discuss the players' demand that they get a slice of the $800,000 World Series television melon,"

- the Washington Redskins reported that a chipped right elbow bone would probably keep "veteran passing wizard" Sammy Baugh from playing against the New York Giants, and

- the National Collegiate Athletic Bureau listed early season total offense leaders, noting, "Johnny Bright, Drake's 190-pound Negro tailback, will smash college football's offensive record if he keeps up his sizzling running and passing streak."[7]

The Republic featured movie ads for:

- "*Sunset Boulevard*" starring William Holden, Gloria Swanson, and Erich von Stroheim at the Phoenix Orpheum,

- "*All Quiet on the Western Front*" starring Lew Ayres and Louis Wolheim at the Rialto,

- "*The Furies*" starring Barbara Stanwyck and Wendell Corey at the Aero, and

---

[7] Later, for the second year in a row, Johnny Bright finished the season as the nation's total offense leader. The following season, in 1951, while again leading the nation in total offense, his college career was ended by a vicious blow to the jaw from Oklahoma A&M's Wilbanks Smith who, a photo sequence suggested, may have targeted him. Fifty-four years later, in 2005, Oklahoma State (formerly Oklahoma A&M) is reported to have formally apologized. Bright later played in the Canadian Football League where at the time of his 1964 retirement he was the league's all-time leading rusher.

- "*Malaya*" starring Spencer Tracey and Jimmy Stewart, playing with "*Bandits of El Dorado*" starring the Durango Kid at the Ramona.

On the eve of the 1950-51 basketball season, the Arizona Republic reported:

- Led by running back Gib Dawson from the Mexican border town of Douglas, Arizona, the Cotton Bowl bound University of Texas finished its football season with just one loss.[8]

- The United Press announced its All-Pacific Coast football team, with a backfield of Washington's Don Heinrich and Hugh McElhenny,[9] California's Johnny Olszewski,[10] and Wilford "Whizzer" White of Arizona State College at Tempe, the nation's leading ground gainer.[11]

---

[8] With 9.6 second speed for 100 yards, Dawson was Arizona's 1948 football Player of the Year. He played in two Cotton Bowls and was named Most Valuable Player in the 1953 College All-Star Game against the Detroit Lions.

[9] In 1956, Heinrich shared the New York Giants quarterback position with Charlie Conerly on a team that won the National Football League championship. Teammates included Frank Gifford and Sam Huff. McElhenny, his University of Washington teammate, is a member of the NFL Hall of Fame.

[10] Olszewski played in two NFL Pro Bowls.

[11] At that time, the University of Arizona in Tucson (hereafter "**UofA**") was Arizona's only university. Since then, Arizona State College at Tempe has become Arizona State University ("**ASU**," referred to herein as "**ASC-Tempe (ASU)**" until renamed) and Arizona State College at Flagstaff has become Northern Arizona University ("**NAU**," referred to herein as "**ASC-Flagstaff (NAU)**" until renamed).

Whizzer White's ASU Sports Hall of Fame plaque reads:

Wilford "Whizzer" White Football / 1947-1950
Named to the 1950 AP second team, White was the first ASU athlete to gain AA mention nationally. He led the nation in rushing and all-purpose running in 1950, and was the first ASU athlete to win NCAA statistical championships. His football jersey, # 33, was retired at the end of his senior season. He was drafted and played for the Chicago Bears.[12]

He was the father of Arizona State and College Hall of Fame quarterback Danny White, whose No. 11 was retired by the ASU Sun Devils. Danny later punted and quarterbacked for the Dallas Cowboys. He was named by Phoenix's Arizona Republic as Arizona's Athlete of the 20th Century.

On December 6, the Republic reported that the Sun Devil athletic board had reaffirmed "its policy in regard to scheduling no team which will not permit the use of Negro athletes."

Also, Republic sports columnist Arnott Duncan reported that "Riney

---

[12] At ASC-Tempe (ASU), Whizzer White was a 1952 backfield teammate of John Henry Johnson, a member of the Pro Football Hall of Fame. With Drake's Johnny Bright, Johnson was one of college football's first premier black running backs. After a single year at ASC-Tempe (ASU) he was the NFL's 18th overall draft pick. He chose instead to play in Canada for a year and was a Canadian Football League predecessor's MVP. In the NFL, with Y.A. Tittle at QB, Joe Perry at fullback and Hugh McElhenny at the other halfback, he became part of the San Francisco 49ers acclaimed "Million Dollar Backfield" -- the only "T Formation" backfield with all four members in the Pro Football Hall of Fame. During a 13-year NFL career, he also played for the Detroit Lions and Pittsburgh Steelers. The Steelers' No. 2 draft pick in 1953, his NFL HOF citation describes him as a "powerful runner, superior blocker."

Salmon, recently resigned president of the Arizona-Texas League, leaves Saturday for Miami [Florida] to invite the minor leagues of baseball to hold their meeting in Phoenix in 1952."[13]

> **The Arizona-Texas League**
>
> The Arizona Texas League, which included teams from Mexico, produced some colorful and talented players.
>
> One of the teams was the Globe-Miami Browns, a Saint Louis Browns farm team. In 1947, one of its pitchers was Ralph "Blackie" Schwamb, who later pitched for the parent team.
>
> In the "*Wrong Side of the Wall: The Life of Blackie Schwamb, the Greatest Prison Baseball Player of All Time*" (Lyons Press, 2004), Eric Stone wrote of the Arizona-Texas League:
>
>> [T]he whole league...was a mixed bag of old guys on their way out; guys who had got into ball during the war and were still trying to hold onto it even though they didn't have a hope in hell of getting back to the big leagues; some young guys from around the Southwest who might or might not make it; and guys like Blackie, disciplinary problems, mostly drunks, who the teams that had signed them were hoping

---

[13] Riney Salmon was a founding member and name partner of Jennings Strouss, the author's law firm. From 1948 through 1950, he was president of baseball's Class C Arizona-Texas League. Reminiscent of George Gipp's dying request in 1920 to "Win just one for the Gipper," in 1926 Riney's brother, John "Button" Salmon, the UofA's student body president, football quarterback and baseball catcher, is said to have asked his coach to "tell the team to bear down" as he lay dying from injuries suffered in an auto accident. Since 1927, "Bear Down" has been the University of Arizona's motto and the theme of its fight song "Bear Down, Arizona."

would straighten up.

.... Wild games were not unusual in the Arizona-Texas League. At Globe, in the second game of the best-of-three playoff, the score was tied four to four in the tenth inning. A Phoenix batter got a double and Billy Martin scored. As he crossed home plate a Globe fan yelled something insulting and before long Martin and the fan were fighting on the field. Then a bunch of fans got into it and soon everyone was throwing punches ....

Reportedly, Schwamb spent far more time in the Shamrock Bar (still there in 2021) than at the ballpark a few blocks away.

After pitching in several games for the St. Louis Browns in 1948, Schwamb, who had been a "leg-breaker" collecting debts for LA mobster Mickey Cohen, robbed and beat to death a doctor who, after a winning day at Hollywood Park, had stopped with his wife at the historic Normandie Card Club in Gardena, California. Convicted, Schwamb was sentenced to life in prison, but he was released in 1960.

In 2008, he was profiled on television's "Amazing Sports Stories."

Mr. Stone's book is a fascinating chronicle of Schwamb's dark life woven into the rich tapestry of Los Angeles's own dark side during the mid-20s, 30s and 40s, and of Schwamb's misspent baseball stops in the minor and major leagues.

In 1947, as a member of the Phoenix Senators, Billy Martin batted a league leading .392. Martin later played in five World Series for the Yankees (Series MVP in 1953) and managed them five different times. He also managed the Twins, Tigers and Rangers.

> Martin had a history of fighting on the field. In the Arizona-Texas League, his fights included several with Clint "Scrap Iron" Courtney, catcher for the Bisbee-Douglas Copper Kings. Described as "pugnacious" and "fiercely combative," Courtney later caught for the Yankees, Browns, Orioles, White Sox, Senators and Athletics from 1951-61. Martin and Courtney continued to fight during their major league careers, for which both were fined.
>
> In 1954, as an Oriole, Courtney hit the first home run in Baltimore's Memorial Stadium. That year, he struck out only seven times in 397 at bats – the fewest since Joe Sewell in 1933.[14]
>
> In 1949, Don Larson, who in 1956 pitched the only perfect game in World Series history, played in seven games for the Globe-Miami Browns.

Beneath the words "Remember Pearl Harbor," the December 7, 1950 Republic pictured the U.S. destroyer Shaw exploding during the Japanese sneak attack nine years before. It noted that 2,335 U.S. servicemen died in the attack.

Against this backdrop an unlikely coach and ethnically diverse group of teenagers put together a basketball team that produced one of the most amazing seasons in the history of high school basketball.[15]

---

[14] Another Arizona-Texas League player, Ozzie Wigman who led the league in home runs, married the author's next-door neighbor, Jean Alden. Her father, Charlie Alden owned Globe's art-deco Fox Theater and later opened the Globe Theater, both of which Ozzie later managed.

[15] In largely scrapbook form, "Sonny" Gomez Pena's *The Mighty Miami Vandals* (Hispanic Institute of Social Studies, 2008) ("**Pena**") is filled with information and perspectives about the 1950-51 Vandals. The book is understood to be out of print but available in local libraries. Those who can access a copy are encouraged to read it. Readers will be well-rewarded by the contemporary reports, photos, sketches, media commentary and contextual information it contains.

The Globe-Miami Area

Miami Copper and Inspiration Consolidated Copper Companies

Pinal Mountains from Globe

Located six miles apart with Miami closest to Phoenix, Globe and Miami sit at about 3,500 feet in the foothills of the Pinal Mountains. Just over 20 miles to the top at 7,848 feet, the Pinals are cold in winter and refreshingly cool in summer. With fir, aspen, pine, oak and juniper, plus deer, javelina, bears, mountain lions and other wildlife, including timber rattlers and an occasional coatimundi at even the highest elevations, they provide popular picnic and recreation areas for the residents below.

In the late 1940s and early 1950s the area economy was largely tied to mining (primarily copper) and ranching.

The two towns were "melting pot" communities with many immigrant families from Mexico and Slavic countries such as Croatia and Serbia. In its Fall 2008 edition, the Globe Miami Times published an article by Bill Norman regarding "the Viches" that read in part:

> America rightfully comes by its nickname of "the great melting pot" largely because of towns like Globe and Miami.
>
> Especially around the turn of the last century, when mining bonanzas were erupting in this part of the world, people from dozens of countries on multiple continents made their way here to seek new lives.
>
> Among the most numerous were those from Slavic regions in Europe, particularly from what are now the countries of Montenegro and Croatia, once Yugoslavian republics, originally part of Austro-Hungary.
>
> They set down roots, and they prospered in many fields of endeavor. Rose Perica married a Mofford and became governor ….
> ….
> The Serbian and Croatian cemeteries in Central Heights bear testament to the lives of the Slavic pioneers ….

With their large Mexican American population, the two towns have spawned many of Arizona's best Mexican food restaurants. Miami's El Rey opened in 1939; and Globe's La Casita opened in 1947. The Globe El Rey opened years before that. The progeny of Globe-Miami families have opened Mexican food restaurants throughout Arizona.

The Town of Miami

In 1950, Miami (pronounced "My-am-ah" by some residents) was essentially a company-owned mining town of about 4,000 (a bit smaller now) in which "Mexicans" were second class citizens.[16] Two mines, Miami Copper Company and Inspiration Consolidated Copper

---

[16] In the language of the day, the term "Mexican" is sometimes used herein to denote those of Mexican heritage, including many of the most admirable people the author has known. The author has been told by several of them that, proud of their heritage, they prefer to be called "Mexican Americans" instead of Latinos, Hispanics or other terms considered by some to be politically correct. *Appendix 6* discusses and quotes from Dr. Christine Marin's observations about the plight of Mexican Americans in Miami at that time.

Company, were the basis of Miami's existence. Located downtown, Miami Commercial was the company store.

At the mines, Mexicans were reportedly paid $1 an hour less than others; and Miles Mortuary reportedly buried Mexicans deeper than others.[17] There was a canyon in lower Miami in which Mexican houses were clustered.[18] Mexicans had their own YMCA and, at Bullion Plaza, they attended their own elementary and junior high school. It was only at the high school level that all students were fully integrated.

Residents owned only the upper several feet of their lots, with the ground below reserved for underground mining. Many of the mostly small, wooden houses were built on hillsides, just a few feet apart. House fires were not uncommon and often spread quickly to neighboring houses.

The busy main street included a J.C. Penney, F.W. Woolworth's, Western Auto, a Ryan-Evans drugstore, and two theaters, the Lyric and the Grand.

Like most, if not all, western mining towns, Miami had "cathouses" – most prominently the 24-room Keystone Hotel, located mid-town near the Catholic Church and the police station. Reportedly, some Miami officials periodically received "good will" payments from the Keystone's owners.

Eventually, like many other Miami buildings, the Keystone burned. In 1996, an enterprising resident sold certified Keystone Hotel bricks for $5 each to raise money for the Boy Scouts. That garnered a lot

---

[17] This and other information was related by Joaquin "Juke" Sanchez, a Miami resident whose parents were Andalusian Spaniards.

[18] See *Grover Canyon*, Samuel P. Echeveste (2004).

of money, and a lot of publicity, including on the front page of Phoenix's Arizona Republic and on prime-time national TV. In an article subtitled "Arizona man sells off whorehouse bricks to support Boy Scouts," the Republic reported that the Keystone Hotel had been closed in 1962 after it took out a Yellow Pages ad offering "woman attendants from noon to 4 a.m. daily." The ad bannered, *"IN ALL ARIZONA … THERE IS ONLY ONE KEYSTONE."*

Bullion Plaza School and Museum

Nearby Globe

Six miles east of Miami, Globe is the county seat of Gila County which, containing 4,796 square miles, includes parts of the San Carlos and Fort Apache Indian Reservations.[19] In 1950 Globe had a population of about 6,500 (a bit larger now). Surrounding ranches and communities added a few thousand more. In addition to the area's copper and turquoise mines, plus some asbestos, silver, gold,

---

[19] The 6th largest state (smaller only than Alaska, Texas, California, Montana and New Mexico), all but one of Arizona's 15 counties is quite large.

lead, zinc, and later uranium mines, its economy was strongly supported by ranchers and to a lesser extent by the San Carlos Apaches whose reservation is nearby.

Globe's main street included a Penney's, Woolworth's, three drugstores and two theaters -- the historic Fox Theater, which was ornately decorated and had an old pre-talkie organ on stage beneath its screen, and the recently built Globe Theater.

Two doors down from the Fox, two U.S. Presidents, "Teddy" Roosevelt (in 1911) and Calvin Coolidge (in 1930), stayed at the historic Old Dominion Hotel while visiting Globe to commemorate the nearby dams on the Salt and Gila Rivers that bear their names.

In the late 1960s, the fully paved south end of Broad Street was converted instead to a dirt street of Reno, Nevada for filming of the "Great White Hope." The movie was a fictionalized version of the racially based hope for a white challenger to take the heavyweight boxing crown from Jack Johnson. From 1908 to 1915 Johnson was the first black man to hold the heavyweight title. He defied social conventions by his brazenly public relationships with white women. In what was termed by some the "Fight of the Century," in 1910, past champion James J. Jeffries had come out of retirement to fight Johnson in Reno but lost.[20]

---

[20] *Unforgivable Blackness: The Rise and Fall of Jack Johnson* is a PBS documentary by Ken Burns based on Geoffrey C. Ward's 2004 book of the same name. In 2018, President Trump posthumously pardoned Johnson who had been convicted in 1913 of violating the federal Mann Act (White Slave Traffic) by unlawfully transporting a white woman across state lines for the purpose of prostitution, debauchery, or "any other immoral purpose." In a May 2018 article published in the *Atlantic*, Jessica Pliley wrote: "[T]he Jack Johnson case was never about vindicating the purity of white womanhood. It always was about punishing a shameless black man for crossing the color line in the bedroom."

Globe, too, had a cathouse -- the White Star Rooms. Painted white, it was a short-stay hotel with a red light next to the front door. It was located on Broad Street between the Firestone store and the Ford Motor Company, almost in the shadow of where Globe's hanging tree (used for just two men) once stood. In earlier years, several other pleasure palaces were located nearby for a few blocks in both directions. If memory serves, the White Star met its demise when, in July of 1954, Pinal Creek flooded buildings on lower Broad Street to depths of up to 10 feet, with the Arizona National Guard called in to screen off a several block area.

Further west toward Phoenix, midway between Miami and Superior at a higher elevation between the two towns, the "Top of the World" was by far the area's best-known cathouse, with university students driving from Tucson and Tempe to patronize it. More than once while at the University of Arizona, the author explained that Globe was "about 20 miles past the Top of the World."

Perhaps because of the "cathouse effect," the author never heard of a sexual assault while he was growing up in Globe; and in our small town such an occurrence would have been gossip fodder about which most would have known.

Ethnic discrimination existed in Globe, too, but not as obviously or as much as in Miami. At the school pool, open during the summers, "whites" swam in the morning, Mexicans in the afternoon. The author later learned from Mexican American classmates that, at night, some of them would climb over the fence and pee in the pool before the whites swam the next morning.

Cobre Valley Country Club, which had a nine-hole course and cost $25 or so to join, was then owned by Inspiration Consolidated Copper Company. It did not allow Mexican members. However, several Mexicans who had somehow become good golfers were provided jobs there and played regularly with the members.

Neither Globe nor Miami had many African Americans. But each had a small school for "coloreds" (the terminology of the day). The author is not aware of anyone having attended the one in Globe during his school years. Two years after the author graduated from Globe High in 1954, Clay Freney, a student-athlete who was extremely well-liked by his fellow students was refused service at a popular local ice cream and sandwich parlor. Other students boycotted. A public apology and change of policy resulted. The author has since learned that there were earlier Globe African American athletes of renown – including Ed Weatherspoon and Cephus Weatherspoon who, with Clay Freney, are members of the Globe High School Hall of Fame established several years ago.

The following two poems by deceased Globe resident Ricardo M. Lucero, a Mexican American, capture the essence of the town in which he and the author grew up:[21]

Mí Roun' Trip

Dedicated To
The Class of 1949-1950
(and anyone else)
(Circa 1947)

Euclid Avenue, an arroyo in a canyon,
becomes a wide boulevard
to hear the inhabitants tell it.
To us that lived there,
Euclid was our circle of life.

Growing up on that street was an adventure.
Henry Guerrero lived on Euclid, so did Meme Soltero.

---

[21] Note the rich ethnic diversity of names and the enriching ethnicities from which they derive. The description is of the Globe the author knew as a young boy and brings vividly to mind visual memories of the places, people and families mentioned who were part of his own life.

And nobody, but nobody could beat ol' brother Hank
at drinking, fighting, laughing and loving life.
Euclid was a strain in that odd-mixture called Globe.

WWII profoundly affected my town.
To a young Mexican youth
whose earliest memory of Anglos
was confrontation, often combat,
life became more confusing.

My older brother had gone to war
to defend this country, which at times
did not seem to want us.
He was taken into the war; he didn't choose it.
He secretly liked Japanese people.
He was often mistaken for one.

The north end of Euclid
was the beginning of Town.
Before me was Willow Street,
the railroad tracks by Dora Bros.,
then Broad Street, and all the action.

Globe High was east from my house
and to get there I'd walk.
Being with familiar people made me feel comfortable,
made me feel secure
Globe was dynamic, fresh, familiar.

Walking between Mitch Vitkovich's and Willie Coppa's
I'd turn right at the real Market,
owned by a Slav named Nick.
Enjoying the aroma of beans from El Cinco de Mayo,
I'd stagger from the odors of Paulino's Saloon
and the Owl Bar.
At the Owl, Gringos and Mexicans almost got along.

Above Jim King's Barber Shop,
were stairs to some mysterious "rooms."

At Bracco's Pharmacy I'd read, but never buy,
comic books 'til Johnny would run me off.

Kitty-corner from the St. Elmo Saloon was George Dee's
bar and adjoining Chinese restaurant,
where some of our teachers secluded themselves,
and like everyone else did their drinking.
Oddly, Johnson the school bus driver drank there too.

There was Zenovich's Market, Jack the baker's,
a car dealer's show place and service department,
Batina's Barber Shop, Powell's Drug Store and the bridge.
A cobbler's shop, later to be Rudy the barber's,
Upton's confectionery,
before it moved uptown across from the Alden Theater,
empty windows, then Joe Fodera's place,
where you drank at your own risk.

Everyone ate at La Casita,
but not everyone drank at the Club Verde.
Putas lived in the rooms above.
More Mexicans than was necessary
had established their reputations in "The Club,"
and it wasn't performing community service.
Sooner or later in Globe you were going to have
to fight your way out of a bar,
but Joe Hinton never had to;
it was said he did things differently.

Close to Jimmy Castle's Auto Body Shop
was Oddonetto's Furniture Store -
owned by Johnny's dad.
Johnny - with a heart as big as him.
We were to meet later in Japan during the Korean war.

Up a way was Ong's Liquor store where
the fortune cookie touched our lives.

There were also "rooms" above Ong's Liquors and
Harry the Greek's little store.

Down a side street by Lantin's Men's Store
were rows of small apartments
where old Chinese men lived.
Dick Coleman and Porter Houseman swore
they all smoked opium!
There too lived wily Roger Kyle,
whose asbestos business
would one day bring ecological grief
to a growing copper town.

Downtown sort of stopped here.
What distinguished it from up-town,
was the high visibility of Mexican cafes,
bars and whore houses,
San Carlos Apaches and Mexicans, and a few poor whites.

After Lantin's was the K and M,
a thriving bar variously owned
by Joe Rais' dad, then the Kenteras - Mickey's family.
Cubitto Jewelers advertised with a tall, bubble-headed,
metal pole, forever painted silver.
The bubble was a huge clock
that stood like a sentinel over half the town.

There was a Four-Square church,
a photography shop and Arizona Savings,
an institution that was the beginning of Chuck Lee's
"inscrutable" accounting system.

Down the next side street was Dr. Harper's office.
Then, the tallest three-story building in the world -
the Elks Club.
My brother Benny learned the BPOE secret rituals:
he cleaned the lodge room after meeting nights.
On the opposite side of the street - more fraternal lodges.

Valley National bank was an awesome building.
We Mexicans believed Tuck White owned it.
There was a pool hall next, operated by a couple of
friendly gamblers named Gobby and Harold.
Further up was Trethewey and Jabour's Home Grocery,
Under the Palms, Shorty Frizell's Barber Shop,
The Mirror,
and Ryans before it was an Evans Drugstore.

A right turn led to the fire station and
just beside it, on the corner down from Penney's
was the police station.
One day my brother Benny
would be a member of that department.

Not forgetting the 8 o'clock bell,
I'd hurry by the Palace Pharmacy,
Given Brothers, and insurance company office
with unusual newsphotos in its windows,
a couple of fraternal lodges, and Gibson's Men's Store.
On the second floor were doctor's offices -
optometrists' I believe.

Then the hall that drew the faithful,
Bill Hardt's Pool Room!
There I met Tommy Long - my Gringo friend
who was as good as me with a cue - and Bud Mooney
who taught me not to rush into a fight.
Next door was Markichevich's Restaurant,
Marko's dad was his own cook,
and then The Lodge
What a grand saloon, completely western.

In the Lodge hardy men drank hard, fought harder,
and just plain acted like men, while other gentlemen
grumbled and gambled at dominoes and cards.
At that corner was another drug store
where Estelle Brooks ground out prescriptions.

Around this corner was a Chinese restaurant
that you climbed down some stairs to get to.

Glancing at the clock above Sullivan's Hardware,
I'd cross Broad Street, cut through a Standard station,
run along Hill Street,
and look the other way at Miles Mortuary.
I'd whip by Patsy Whitlock's, Kellner's Tiger's Den,
Gundry's Texaco,
and the school with almost a school yard, Hill Street.
Then I'd dart by Wyant's store,
speed past Elinor Hersey's, John Bayer's,
and collapse at the side door to Globe High.

My days in school were filled with misadventure,
absenteeism, and abject disregard for rules.
In spite of myself, I was tolerated
and had more friends than I deserved.
In time, belligerence and delinquency,
bordering on the criminal, had me expelled,
and brought to an end my academic career.
I had started as vice-president
to Bob Shaw as a freshman,
and didn't make it through the 11th.
I managed to stay out of Ft. Grant,
though later I would work there, under Steve Vukcevich.
My first son would be born there.

And I remember the names, the threatening names,
that now sound beautiful!
Cromer, Stevenson, Clements, Miller,
Knox, Peckovich, Rittschof,
Helmke (what a great man),
Zona Hazelwood and Cubitto.

Vickrey, Mozelle Wood, Farmer, Hachtel,
Strong, Anderson, White, Pendantic Pothoff,
the academic Blanch Kennedy,

the logician Miss Davies,
who taught algebra and understood symbols.

And Blondie Price,
whose name connoted augury and power.
He had the keys to everything
and he could get you jobs helping him
Saturdays and after school - Blondie, school custodian.
To young Chicanos, he was a big man.

After school I'd return to my barrio
the same route, on the opposite side of the street.
Going by the band hall where the buses parked,
I'd turn right, charting a path to the post office,
by way of the Mormon Church that stood staring at the
K of C Hall.

I'd aggravate the hell out of the idle postmen
by asking them to snap open my family's P.O. box.
If I wasn't in a hurry,
I'd cross the street by the Baptist church,
that massive temple built from blocks of caliche.
At the "employment" office I would instinctively
turn my face and hold it all the way
by the Sheriff's Department, past Clyde Shute's office
and never straighten my head
'til I got to Woolworth's,
where some of us did our Christmas shoplifting.

Close by was Globe Theatre,
and next, the office of the Arizona Record, a newspaper
of far superior journalism than the Silverbelt;
it was, after all, at that time published in GLOBE!
And at that corner an old hotel.
The Greyhound Bus Depot was once in that hotel.
It was when Pete Oddonetto, Ray Arona, Jim Troglia,
and Jimmy Fairfield returned from the war.

Remember the Arizona Bushmasters?
Marko Babich was in the horse cavalry, remember?
A right turn led to two institutions, whose business was
transmitting messages-
Mountain Bell and the Salvation Army.
Jean Kling's dad was a big man at Mountain Bell,
ask Roscoe.

If I could, I'd stop at the Arizona Bakery,
owned by Jeanette Caretto's family,
and overdose on day-old pastry.
There was Nella's Flower Shop
where Ophelia's sister-in-law Jo worked.
It was close to a fabric shop, and Usher's Radio Repair,
Gene's dad's shop.
There was a shoeshine stand near there,
owned by J.B. something or other - a black man.
I remember him well, he lived on my street.

There was Sears and then Hachtel's Tonto Hotel.
If you turned right on this corner
you had a hell of a climb up Mesquite Street,
dangerously steep.

I got acquainted with back-breaking work
setting pins in a bowling alley on the next corner.
Then there was Rayes' Eagle Grocery.
My mother bought groceries there
with coupon books sold to us
by the Eagle Grocery to be used for purchases
in the Eagle Grocery only. A little like the company store,
except they delivered. George was the driver.

Lido Lopez was a well-liked apprentice meat cutter there
before he served in the Navy during the war,
only to return and be tragically consumed
by over-consumption.

Paul Bejar's mother worked there
in the fruit and vegetable section.

Griffith Cleaners was near J.T. Lewis Paint Store.
It was by Fred Sunfield's Standard Furniture,
oddly situated across the street from Oddonetto's.
I seem to remember a Cadillac dealership around here.

Further down was Rais' Market - Mary Frances' family.
Then Bustamonte's Body Shop
and a two-story building - The White Star -
with yet more sporting girls on the second floor.
An auto parts store was on the street floor near a
vaguely remembered Barclay's Feed and Grain store
where as a younger boy
I'd line up on cold mornings to buy baby chicks.
Albert Rivera's cleaners was around here somewhere.
Just before the bridge was Fred Fritz's Texaco.

A concrete walkway up the right side of the creek
became long steep stairs on a hillside.
Up there lived the Canizales, Cienfuegos, John Phillips,
and Clarence Murray. Remember "Tiny"?
Clutching his books, dancing and shouting in Russian?
Clarence, our very own Bolshevik.

Passing the bridge was Al Ledbetter's Richfield station.
Next was another two-story building
with another whorehouse.
In those days whorehouses operated openly in Globe.
And in Miami.
Remember the Keystone Rooms? Top o' the World?
Now that was class.

In my younger days I had shined shoes and sold papers
on the streets and in the saloons of Globe.
About once a month i would clean and shine
every pair of shoes of every Girl living in those places.

I have never forgotten the lonely, pretty girl who
would sadly tell me of her family whom she loved -
but who had rejected her.
And one night she leaped from her window.
She was seriously hurt only,
and now had another heavy pain: she would
live with an unsuccessful attempt at dying.

I loved the smell of baking bread as I walked past
Quality Jack's glowing ovens.
From Sach's Ford Motors (wasn't it Maher's before?)
I would walk straight up Hackney past the tracks
at Solomon Wichersham's wholesale warehouse.
On Hackney was Joe Giacoma's Store
and the Rev. Banuelos' Mexican Presbyterian Church.

By the Tapia's compound near the ball park,
I would go over a hump that joined Hackney with Euclid.
Fred Barela lived on this mound,
close to Carmen! Of course.

Up a trail between houses I'd pass by the Reyes'
and the Lopez', a large pioneer family.
Legend had it that Doña Cecilia
had sheltered and fed Geronimo
as he fled from pursuing cavalry.
Four of the brothers were Lido, Chido, Mato, and Chato!
Not in that order,
but Bunch Guerrero spoke of them that way.
He liked to have their names rhyme.

Then I'd reach my house on top of my hill
not far from Tony Chiono's home
completing my trip!

Forever I'll remember Buena Vista, Ruiz Canyon,
Ice House and Six Shooter Canyons too.
Blake Street, Noftsger Hill School, East Globe,

the 400 section, and many more memories of my youth.
Nobody has yet explained how Gil Barela's house
was built in a creek and was never washed away.
Mexicans quietly accepted it as just another one of
Globe's Miracles.

To once more dive into Maurel's swimming pool
and the school pool too.
Remember Strukan's grocery store,
Slough's market, Mary's Place, T.J. Longs?
Globe-Miami games and fights,
basketball games and brawls?

We fought everybody, we befriended everyone.
Growing up in GLOBE, how beautiful,
how fortunate we were....

Presented at the
Class of -49 - 50 Reunion
rml ~ 1980
Used with permission of Benny Lucero

The "Bushmasters" to whom Ricardo referred was the Arizona National Guard that, activated during WWII, fought in New Guinea and in retaking the Philippines. General MacArthur said of the Bushmasters: "No greater fighting combat team has ever deployed for battle."

Belying the adage that one can't go home, the author has always felt that he can go home to Globe. He does so repeatedly. Given a choice, with the same circumstances, teachers, coaches and peers, without hesitation he would grow up there again.

¿Illusiones?

We're back
once again connected
ignoring age, denying time

Euphoric.
We gather in fondness
to laugh, to touch
to talk of life
of me and you and youth
to cry and lose ourselves
in time.

Some restless nights
we find ourselves in Globe;
trace those narrow silent streets
parched arroyos, awesome canyons, grand Pinals
searching for our self
in that old dominion
where our dreams fit
in that expanse.

We're proprietary about our copper culture.
Our 'mother lode' is there
where spewing sulfur smoke
wounds pristine silica skies
that cushion the harshness
of fertile red hills
which stare through open shafts
and gutted caves -
a land of contrasts
that breeds gratitude
and strength.

Here we stand
fewer in number, greater in substance
and style.

Our missing mates and absent friends
are in another realm
beyond some nether place, some otherwhere.
They're just as here
as we are there.

> We'll celebrate ourselves,
> resentfully re-enter time
> and then
> our psyches will be bruised again
> 'til we return to dream of them;
> to love and feel complete again
> in Globe.

Used with permission of Benny Lucero.

With a like diversity of surnames, many the same, similar poems could portray Miami's ethnic diversity and the pride and sense of community of those living there.

For his 50th class reunion, the author compiled his own list of memories, which read in part:

'54 Memories

Slag, turning the western sky orange at night, the huge stack at Inspiration, spewing smoke; the taste of sulfur.

The Old Dominion and Pioneer Hotels; and the White Star, Keystone and Top of the World.

The Fox and Globe Theaters; and the drive-in between Globe and Miami.

Upton's (upper and lower); vanilla root beers.

The Eagle, Pay-N-Take It, Hillstreet, and East Globe groceries.

Willard Shoecraft, indomitable, with no legs hopping about downtown.

Billie Shoecraft, Willard's attractive blond wife, who later thought Agent Orange had crazed her neighbor's cow.

The shootings in the Owl Buffet.

Mrs. Tewksbury's tamale cart, going house to house.

A Welsh woman, who occasionally came through the neighborhood selling pasties.

Charles Collins, the saddle maker.

Our freshman football equipment consisting of shoes with bolts on the bottom but no cleats until the varsity got new ones and gave us their old ones, and my uniform (better than most) that included a helmet with the suspension straps inside partially torn loose and hip pads that I had to strap on with a rope.

"Wink," who supplied us newspapers for a nickel to sell for a dime.

Noftsger Hill, East Globe and Hill Street Schools.

Max Spilsbury, for whom I would have done anything.

John Pavlich, who taught us that nice guys can win, who humorously described those who could skillfully use both hands as "amphibious," and who repeatedly said:
- "If you see a ball rolling around on the field fall on it, it might be the one we're playing with."
- "I saw someone snap a towel in the locker room once, and an eyeball went rolling across the floor."
- "What time did you get in last night? What time did you get up and go home?"
- "There's nothing wrong with my old pickup I couldn't fix by jacking up the radiator cap and driving a new pickup under it."

The Western Union, with its big clock inside.

Charlie Alden's strings of big red and green theater lights, decorating his tall cedar trees from top to bottom at Christmas – visible all over town, and right next to our house on Sycamore Street.

The '50-51 basketball Vandals – undefeated, with three players in succession breaking the state single-game scoring record and setting a national scoring record of 130 points against Morenci.

Our '53 football Tigers – small, quick, and high-scoring, with only a single 1-point loss.

Our English teachers (Mrs. Barnett, Miss Potthoff and Miss Kennedy), who taught me far more than I realized.

Marie Hachtel, who taught me to type, with whom I worked to publish the *Papoose* (our school weekly), and who saved my ass from Miss Kennedy who sent me out of her class for inattention.

Max Oliger ("Don't ever kiss anyone's ass, but if patting it will help use both hands!").

Sanchez's band ("Tencia, I love you so").

The Mambo, and the Miami girls who could really do it.

Lupe Provencio whose sexy dancing drove the teachers nuts – who could forget!

"Chito" Castellanos, one of my heroes – at 139 pounds, breaking his collarbone and Coolidge's 300-pound fullback's ankle; then riding the team bus back to Globe; and a year or two before that getting four teeth knocked out at practice.

Dominic "Pusso" Renon, with shoulders like aircraft carriers.

"G" Hill; Slaughterhouse Hill; Moonshine Hill; Wheatfields; the empty hangers at Cutter – our places of "Paradise by the Dashboard Light."

The dirt jalopy racetrack and Tucson's "Wild Bill" Cheesbourg who violently slammed his car around the track and later raced at Indy where in 1957 he set a record by passing 17 cars on the first lap.

The CCC Camp, Pioneer Pass, Tuxedo and Mud Tank; the Six Shooter Canyon trail cabin; Signal Peak; Pinal Peak and lady bugs; Oak Flats; Seven-Mile Wash.

The old road to Superior; and the one through Salt River Canyon – when, without side rails, they were narrow, dangerous and scary.

The old Hill Street Gym – where Gil Barela once tipped in a jump ball from the free throw line, and where the overhanging balcony at one end was like a 6th and 7th defender.

The Nob Hill Grocery (still there about 81 years later), where my grandmother sometimes let me go alone when we lived on Mesquite Street and I was about 4-years old.

A friend hit in the ear by a shotgun pellet that barely missed his eye as ducks flew from a Tonto Creek pond we had brilliantly approached in pairs from opposite sides to outsmart the ducks.

The nearby lakes, Roosevelt, Apache and at Coolidge Dam.

Globe's fire horn, blown every night at 9:30 pm as a curfew to which no one paid attention.

The 1950-51 Miami Vandals

1951 CONCENTRATOR

Presented by the Students
of
MIAMI HIGH SCHOOL
Miami, Arizona

(Photo: Miami High School Yearbook)
(Miami Players: Lupe Acevedo and Eli Lazovich)

Coach Kivisto

Background

Of first-generation Finnish descent, Ernie Kivisto grew up speaking his native language "on the wrong side of the tracks" in Ironwood, Michigan (just south of Lake Superior near the Wisconsin border). His son, Bob, states that "Coach" was obsessed with basketball and walked to school in the snow so he could play after classes.

As a college sophomore, he played at Marquette University in 1942-43. Then, as a Marine trainee during WWII, he played for Notre Dame during his 1943-44 junior year.[22] After his discharge from the Marines, he returned to Marquette as a senior for the 1945-46 season. He then played AAU ball in Milwaukee before beginning his coaching career.

---

[22] Johnny Lujack, a freshman basketball team-mate at Notre Dame, was the starting guard. Later, with Lujack at quarterback the Notre Dame football team went undefeated in his final two years and he won the 1947 Heisman Trophy.

Coaching Career

The word "legendary" has been used often to describe coach Kivisto and his career. After his death, headings and commentary included:

- 2003, in the Quad-City Times (Davenport, Iowa): "Coaching legend Kivisto dies,"

- 2010, in the Paddock Publications Daily Herald columnist Jeff Long referred to Kivisto as "the legendary, Hall of Fame basketball coach,"

- 2012, in an Aurora Trib article titled *East Gym Renamed after Kivisto on Saturday* Clayton Muhammad wrote: "The legendary Ernie Kivisto coached from 1967 through the 1981-82 season at East Aurora High School," and

- 2020, for the Enterprise Newspapers, Drake Skleba wrote: "Kivisto was the legendary IHSBCA Hall of Fame head coach of the Tomcats from 1967-1981."

Arriving at Miami in 1947, Coach Kivisto had a 95-8 win/loss record during his four seasons there, with season records of:

1947-48: 22-3
1948-49: 22-3
1949-50: 24-2
1950-51: 27-0

During his tenure at Miami, the Vandals won 51 consecutive home games. He next coached at **United Township High School in East Moline, Illinois** and then at **Aurora East in Illinois**. Summarizing his career, his East Aurora Hall of Fame tribute reads in part:

 ## Ernie Kivisto
(1923 – 2003)
Head Coach of the East Aurora Tomcats
(1967 – 1982)

Ernie Kivisto grew up playing basketball in the Upper Peninsula of Michigan in the days prior to World War II, the son of an immigrant iron worker from Finland. In 1941, he received All-State Honors during his senior year at Luther Wright High School in Ironwood.

During college, he played for Marquette University in 1943 and 1946, and at the University of Notre Dame in 1944, being moved back and forth while being in the U.S. Marines reserves during the war.

His coaching career began in the late 1940's, coaching a Semi-Professional team for a couple of years, before getting the Head Coaching position at Miami High School in Miami, Arizona. There, in 1951, Ernie's team went 27-0 and won the Arizona State Championship, set state and national records….

After that season, Ernie became the Head Coach at United Township High School in East Moline, Illinois. He had many great teams at East Moline and is an enshrined member of the United Township Hall of Fame. Ernie's teams won 232 games at East Moline, and his son, Bob, as a freshman, once scored 52 points in a varsity game.

In 1967, Ernie came to East Aurora High School. In that first season, the Tomcats won the Upstate 8 Conference Championship. The 1969 and 1970 teams added to that glory, again winning conference titles, along with Regional, Sectional, and Super-Sectional Championships.

Like his older brother in 1968, Tom Kivisto was named a High School All American in 1970, once scoring 56 points in a game. Both of the boys went on to start at the University of Kansas, where Bob led his 1971 Jayhawks to the Final Four, and Tom led the 1974 Kansas men to the Final Four.

Ernie continued to have great teams through the 1970's and early 1980's, going downstate 3 times and winning conference titles in '68, '70, '72, '74, '78, '79, '80 and '81. The 1972 team, at the state tournament, set an Illinois record of scoring 346 points in the 4 games downstate....

In his time at East Aurora, Ernie also became known for his summer basketball camps, which drew huge numbers of young players, and for his speaking engagements and clinic instruction.

He also is remembered for his mannerisms, humor, and enthusiasm. Those who played for him have many stories of the way Coach Kivisto motivated his teams, worked them hard, and kept them excited for basketball.

Ernie is a member of the Illinois Basketball Coaches Association Hall of Fame with 544 wins in the State of Illinois. He's also enshrined in the Ironwood High School Hall of Fame and the Michigan Basketball Hall of Fame. He and his 1951 team are inducted in the Arizona Basketball Hall of Fame, and, of course, he is in the East Aurora High School Hall of Fame.

He and Bob and Tom have all been included in the "Faces in the Crowd" articles in Sports Illustrated Magazine.

In 1979, Ernie was selected as the National Coach of the Year by the National High School Athletic Coaches Association....

Like many legends, Coach Kivisto's may have partially morphed into a mythology of hyperbole. His coaching record and even a complete list of the last schools at which he coached are difficult to pin down. After his 2003 death, Steve Tappa of the quad cities' Dispatch-Rock City Argus noted: "The 1979 National High School Coach of the Year, Kivisto claimed to be among the elite group of high-school boys basketball coaches to win more than 1,000 games, though friends and foes alike questioned the accuracy of his record-keeping." Whatever the precise numbers, Coach Kivisto's coaching career was among the most successful ever.

A charter inductee into the Illinois Basketball Coaches Association Hall of Fame while still coaching at East Aurora, his IBCAHOF bio reads in part:

> "One of the most dynamic coaches in the game," is the only way to describe Kivisto from East Aurora High School. A developer of 27 All-State Players and seven high school All-American players, Coach Kivisto had a fantastic record of 545 wins and only 177 losses in 28 years of coaching (at the time of his 1973 hall of fame induction) ….

Two of Coach Kivisto's sons, Bob and Tom, were among the All-Americans he developed.

After his death, the Illinois Senate commemorated his coaching and personal achievements with a Resolution stating: "[H]e will be remembered for his end-to-end pressure defense and [rapid fire] offense." The Resolution cited him for his work "with children with Down syndrome, mental disabilities, and physical disabilities."[23]

---

[23] For more about Coach Kivisto see *Appendix 1*.

Miami's Team

<u>Standing</u>: Coach Kivisto, Hector Jacott, Eli Lazovich, Rudy Moreno, Leigh Larson, Al Lobato, Jesus Romero (manager)
<u>Kneeling</u>: Lupe Acevedo, Dickie Vargas, Fito Trujillo, Elias Delgadillo, Andy Rumic

In 2013, Copper Area News Publishers reported:

> In 1951, three years before the Supreme Court banned segregation in public schools, in the tiny mining town of Miami in southeast Arizona, a sports legend was born.
>
> That year, The Mighty Vandals went undefeated, broke nine national high school records and 18 state records and won the state championship. The team of mostly Mexican teens from the poor side of Miami, Arizona, were led by Coach Ernie Kivisto, a Midwestern transplant, who coached the team from 1947 until their championship win.

The Vandals' roster included just 10 players -- five guards, three forwards, and two centers. Yet, during the team's 20 regular season games, they reportedly called just one timeout, to their opponent's 99.[24] They called two more timeouts during the seven-game post-season play.

All, including the coach, were from immigrant families -- seven from Mexico; one from Serbia; one from Croatia; one from Scandinavia. The coach's family was from Finland.[25]

In 2002, long-time National Basketball Association referee Tommy Nunez helped establish the Arizona Hispanic Sports Hall of Fame. The Mexican American members of the Miami Vandals' 1950-51 team were inducted during its inaugural event.

---

[24] *"The Amazing Miami Vandals: Run! Shoot! Score,"* Arizona Prep (December 1974).

[25] For individual player profiles see *Appendix 2*.

The Regular Season

After the preceding season's disappointing state tournament loss to powerful Nogales, which had won the State Class B Championship in 1949 and in the 1950 final lost by 3 points, Miami and its fans had high hopes for the 1950-51 season.

At its outset, Arizona Republic sports caricaturist Kearney Edgerton (the "Edge") featured Coach Kivisto and called Miami's Vandals the "odds-on favorites for the State Class-B Championship." He noted that the Vandals had won 42 straight games on their home court and that Coach Kivisto's 1948 Vandal team set a national scholastic record by "averaging 70.1 points per game." He also credited Coach Kivisto with having previously "coached St. Ambrose High of Ironwood, Mich, to an undefeated nine-game season" in football.

The 1950-51 season opened against the ominous backdrop of the Korean War that had begun a few months before and cast a pall over the futures of those about to graduate. The division of the Korean peninsula had occurred at the end of World War II following Japan's August 1945 surrender. Creating North and South Korea, the division ended Japan's 35-year rule. Divided by the 38th parallel, the United States and the Soviet Union each occupied a portion of the country. As reported in on-line History:

> On June 25, 1950, the Korean War began when some 75,000 soldiers from the North Korean People's Army poured across the 38th parallel, the boundary between the Soviet-backed Democratic People's Republic of Korea to the north and the pro-Western Republic of Korea to the south. This invasion was the first military action of the Cold War. By July, American troops had entered the war on South Korea's behalf. As far as American officials were concerned, it was a war against the forces of international communism

itself. After some early back-and-forth across the 38th parallel, the fighting stalled and casualties mounted …. Meanwhile, American officials worked anxiously to fashion some sort of armistice with the North Koreans. The alternative, they feared, would be a wider war with Russia and China–or even, as some warned, World War III. Finally, in July 1953, the Korean War came to an end. In all, some 5 million soldiers and civilians lost their lives during the war. The Korean peninsula is still divided today.[26]

Because of a forfeited first game, the Vandals opened their season a week after most other teams were in action.

According to the Republic, Phoenix Carver had become "the team to fear in Class B" after winning two games the preceding weekend. Carver's coach announced that Charlie Christopher, a freshman, would play with the varsity as well as with the jayvees.[27]

However, Republic columnist Ray Silvius wrote:

> [W]ith poker-face and steady hand, I'll point yonder toward the hills and say: Miami High is loaded again and this may be the year that the Vandals will be too hot to handle….
>
> The Vandals will be after their 41st consecutive home

---

[26] The war had a pervasive impact. For example, the Arizona National Guard was activated and "Fuzzy" Ambos, a neighbor of the author who lived just three doors away suffered serious wounds. A husband and father, he was the Superior Court Clerk. His wife performed his duties during his absence.

[27] Later termed "one of the greatest athletes ever developed in Arizona high school ranks," Charlie Christopher died at age 20 during surgery after breaking his wrist while playing as a freshman in a varsity basketball game at ASC-Tempe (ASC). See *Appendix 7*.

victory when they play host to St. Johns in their season beginner Saturday.... The copper country kids won't have the advantages of a new gym as originally planned -- construction of theirs has been held up -- but as far as experienced manpower is concerned they have sufficient.... Eli Lazovich, first team all-stater, who scored 529 points last season, Lupe Acevedo, also an all-stater, Rudy Moreno and Hector Jacott all are back from last year's team, a club that lost only its opener and to Nogales in the state tournament semifinals.... The Vandals will be tall and will have lots of scoring ability.... Looks like a good bet ....

In Other News

That week, in college football, the Republic reported that Arizona State's Whizzer White, "the greatest back in the state of Arizona's history," would play in San Francisco's East-West Shrine Game and that he had been named second team All-American by the Associated Press.

Whitney Martin of the Associated Press reported that the National Association of Women Artists had selected New York Yankee Yogi Berra has having one of the 10 most stimulating faces in America "because it stimulates women's subconscious yearning for the Neanderthal man."

Week One:

Miami's first game was to be with the Fort Thomas Apaches to the east on Highway 70 toward El Paso, but the Apaches forfeited.

> **Fort Thomas and the San Carlos Apache Reservation**
>
> On the Gila River east of Globe near Safford, Camp Thomas was

established to move the Chiricahua Apaches to the San Carlos Reservation. It was designated as a fort in 1882 and became the regimental headquarters for the 3d U.S. Cavalry. It remained an active military post until after Geronimo's surrender in 1886. The adjacent town of Fort Thomas is said to have been filled with brothels and saloons.

The San Carlos Apache Reservation begins a few miles west of Fort Thomas and its western boundary is just a few miles east of Globe. The reservation covers a large area and is rich in minerals, wildlife and history. On multiple occasions, Geronimo was brought to San Carlos only to grow restless, leave with other Apaches, and pursue depredations in southeastern Arizona, southwestern New Mexico and northern Mexico. Famed Apache Scout, Al Sieber, who was involved in Geronimo's next to last "capture," is buried in Globe.

Friday, December 8, 1950

Miami	Wins Forfeit
Fort Thomas	Loses Forfeit

The following night, St. Johns became the first of Miami's victims. The preceding year in Miami's first game, St. Johns had beaten Miami by one point, 40-39 – Miami's only loss during the 1949-50 regular season. [28]

St. Johns

A Mormon community on the Little Colorado River, St. Johns is the

---

[28] Fito Trujillo related that, in 1949-50 when he was a junior, Miami suited up 12 players on its road trips. He was not one of the 12 but made the trip to St. Johns because Lupe Acevedo was injured. He suited up in Lupe's uniform, but at halftime Miami was losing and Coach Kivisto had Lupe suit up, leaving Fito without a uniform.

County Seat of Apache County in northeastern Arizona.

Notables who grew up there included Secretary of the Interior Stuart Udall (1961-69), two Chief Justices of the Arizona Supreme Court, Morris Udall, an Arizona lawyer and Congressman who ran for President, and Rex Lee who began his career as a contemporary of the author at Jennings Strouss.

Rex was a remarkable person – friendly, upbeat, brilliant and fair-minded, with a smile that lit up the room.[29] Before joining Jennings Strouss, Rex clerked for Supreme Court Justice Byron White. In 1971 at age 36, Rex became the Founding Dean of Brigham Young University's Law School. In 1981 at age 46, President Reagan appointed him United States Solicitor General. In 1989 at age 54, he became Dean of BYU. Beginning at Jennings Strouss, Rex argued 59 cases before the Supreme Court. He died of cancer at age 61. Utah Senator Mike Lee is the son of Rex and his wife Janet.

Saturday, December 9, 1950

Miami   78
St. Johns 41

Paced by Eli Lazovich's 22 points and Fito Trujillo's 20, the Vandals opened their season with a 37-point win over St. Johns. It was the Vandals' 41st consecutive home court win.

---

[29] Another distinguished public servant who joined Jennings Strouss just out of the UofA law school was Jon Kyl, who served as a United States Senator for Arizona from 1995 to 2013, and again in 2018. In 2010, *Time* magazine named him one of the 100 most influential people *in the world*. Jon and his wife, Caryll, are long-time family friends. Since 1964, Jennings Strouss has also spawned a 9th Circuit Court of Appeals Judge, two United States District Court Judges, three Arizona Court of Appeals Judges, multiple Arizona Superior Court Judges, a Phoenix Mayor and two U.S. Representatives.

In Other Basketball News:

On Saturday morning, the Republic reported that Class A Phoenix West High School had nosed out cross-town rival North High 32-31.[30]

That night, Globe beat Pima 46-38; and the Class B Nogales Apaches beat Class A St. Mary's in Phoenix 37-36. The Republic noted that it was the Apaches' second win in three starts, with a loss to Tucson (then Arizona's largest high school) the preceding week.

On Monday, December 11, the Republic reported that the Nogales Apaches had beaten the Carver Monarchs 51-50 at Carver on Saturday night. Buddy Islas of Nogales and Hadie Redd of Carver each scored 21 points.

On Thursday, December 14, the Arizona Silver Belt (published weekly in Miami) reported that the development of Fito Trujillo "who had barely stayed on the team last year" was "an object lesson in achievement through hard work." It noted that at 5'10" Trujillo had recovered 24 rebounds in the St. Johns game after having been rated about 10th among returning lettermen. The Silver Belt reported that, while working at a grocery store during the summer, Fito had practiced on his own at an outdoor court 20 to 25 hours a week during his lunch hour and when he was not working.

In Other News

In Korea that night, three regiments of the 1st Marine Division and units of the Army completed their desperate and remarkable breakout from the Chosin Reservoir in Korea.[31]

---

[30] Note the low scores that were prevalent at that time.

[31] After General Douglas McArthur's brilliantly conceived and stunningly

On Sunday December 10:

- The Associated Press reported that Drake's Johnny Bright set three national season records during the past football season, breaking the total offense record held by Frank Sinkwich of Georgia, the record for touchdowns produced held by Charlie "Choo Choo" Justice of North Carolina and Stan Heath of Nevada, and the record for average total offense per game. Babe Parilli of Kentucky and Whizzer White of Arizona State also broke the record for touchdowns produced.

- The AP quoted Joe Louis as "not interested in meeting Ezzard Charles (to whom Louis had lost his heavyweight boxing championship) again."

- Republic cartoonist Kearney Egerton portrayed Globe's Mark "Marko" Markichevich as expected to "carry a large part of ASC at Tempe's victory hopes against Miami of Ohio in the Phoenix Kiwanis Club's Salad Bowl game New Year's Day."

In the Thursday, December 14 Republic:

- The AP reported that Wisconsin Senator Joseph McCarthy, whose intense effort to expose Communist subversion in our post WWII institutions was termed "McCarthyism" by many in the media, had assaulted columnist Drew Pearson at the "plush" Sulgrave Club in Washington, D.C. Pearson had been

---

successful landing at Inchon on the west coast of Korea, and the liberation of Seoul and rapid push north that followed, in mid-October thousands of Chinese soldiers had unexpectedly poured into North Korea, trapping the fast-moving American forces in the freezing winter. The horrific account of the entrapment by overwhelming Chinese forces and the breakout that followed is compellingly told in *Breakout: The Chosin Reservoir Campaign, Korea 1950*, Martin Russ (Penguin Books 2000).

critical of McCarthy's high-profile hunt for Communists. California Senator Richard Nixon allegedly intervened to end the encounter.

- The AP reported that the New York Boxing Association had awarded the Edward J. Nell memorial plaque to welterweight champion Sugar Ray Robinson, "considered by many expert observers the greatest fighter of the generation." Nell was a "former Associated Press boxing writer who was killed in 1937 while serving as a war correspondent in Spain." Past winners had included Jack Dempsey, Billy Conn, Henry Armstrong, Joe Lewis, Barney Ross, Benny Leonard, former New York mayor James J. Walker, Tony Zale, Gus Lesnevich, and Ike Williams. At age 30, Sugar Ray's record was 117-1-2. The loss was to middleweight champion Jake LaMotta [the "Raging Bull"] whom Sugar Ray defeated four times.

- An AP poll found that most of the nation's football writers and sportscasters who responded believed "television, if left unbridled, will spell the doom of college football."

Week Two:

Week two featured games against the mining community of Superior located 30 miles west on the way to Phoenix and against the Mormon farming and junior college community of Thatcher located 70 miles east.

Superior

An underground copper mining community, Superior was later the setting for the esoteric movie *U Turn*, directed by Oliver Stone, with Sean Penn, Jennifer Lopez, Nick Nolte, Billy Bob Thornton, Joaquin Phoenix, Powers Boothe and Jon Voight.

> **Friday, December 15, 1950**
>
> Miami   63
> Superior   41

After leading 26-11 at the half despite Lazovich having played only part of the first quarter before crashing into the wall of the Panther's short gym and Acevedo having been sat down to rest an injured leg, the Vandals were led to victory by Rudy Moreno with 19 points.[32]

> **Thatcher**
>
> Located on the Gila River, Thatcher is the home of Eastern Arizona College.
>
> It was the birthplace of Jess Mortenson, who set the world decathlon record in 1931 and from 1951 to 1961 coached the University of Southern California to seven NCAA track and field championships. During his 11-year tenure at USC his teams were 64-0 in dual meet competition.

> **Saturday, December 16, 1950**
>
> Miami   87
> Thatcher   39

Winning by 48 points with every team member scoring, Acevedo led the scoring with 23, followed by Moreno with 15 and by Lazovich and Trujillo with 14 each. Miami won by 48 points.

---

[32] A couple of years later, while running full-speed to block a break-away layup from behind at the same end, the author, too, crashed into the wall that was below a stage, but although stunned wasn't hurt.

Week Three:

Week three involved a 200-mile foray by Miami to two Mexican border towns. Both had traditionally strong athletic programs.

Bisbee

Located 23 miles southeast of Tombstone and a few miles north of Naco, Mexico, Bisbee was at one time the largest town between St. Louis and Los Angeles. As of several years ago, its baseball field was the oldest in the country still being used.

Home to the once-rich Copper Queen Mine, its copper related minerals are seen in museums world-wide. It is especially noted for its Bisbee Blue turquoise.

In 1883, Bisbee was the site of the infamous "Bisbee Massacre," a robbery gone bad that resulted in four deaths, including a pregnant woman. One of the perpetrators was later taken from jail and lynched. Five more were legally hanged.

Bisbee was also the site of 1917's "Bisbee Deportation" in which a group of about 1,300 striking miners was rounded up, put on a train, and shipped to New Mexico.

Thursday, December 21, 1950

Miami   74
Bisbee   35

Playing at Bisbee before a packed crowd of 1,500, Trujillo led Miami with 22 points, followed by Lazovich with 17.

The Silver Belt reported that, "with the Nogales coach and team in the stands, Coach Kivisto used his first team for only half the game." In an upset, the Nogales Apaches had eliminated the Vandals from the state tournament the year before. Limiting the play of its starters, Miami defeated the Pumas by 39 points.

Nogales

Sixty-nine miles south of Tucson, Nogales, Arizona, and its Mexican twin, Nogales, Mexico, straddle the Arizona-Mexico border.

With bullfights, Canal Street (a red-light district), cheap liquor and other attractions, Nogales, Mexico was a popular destination for male students at the UofA in Tucson and at ASC-Tempe (ASU) further north. Students at the latter, located in the Phoenix suburb of Tempe, derisively referred to Tucson (where the UofA was located) as "Nogales Junction."

At state the year before, Miami lost its second game of the entire 1949-50 season to Nogales, led by Oscar Islas and Porfirio "Buddy" Islas. Both were named 1st team All-State, as were Miami's Lupe Acevedo and Eli Lazovich, both juniors.[33] In the 1950-51 season, having already beaten Phoenix St. Mary's, Nogales (led by Frank Gomez who would later be named 1st team All-State) was again a powerhouse.

<u>Friday, December 22, 1950</u>

Miami   56
Nogales 50

---

[33] Also a junior, Carver's Hadie Redd was selected to the 1950 All-State 1st team. Redd, Acevedo and Lazovich would again be selected 1st team All-State in 1951. Thus, the 1951 state title game featured three two-time 1st team All-Staters.

Miami trailed Nogales at the end of the first quarter and at the half. Tied 41-41 after the third quarter, the Vandals took the lead during the first four minutes of the final quarter and then froze the ball. The Silver Belt reported that "for three and a half minutes Nogales never touched the ball." Acevedo led Miami with 18 points. Lazovich scored 12 and Trujillo 10.

Week Four:

The Silver Belt reported that Flagstaff (with a 5-2 record) and Winslow (with a 6-1 record) were Miami's next opponents. Both were located on well-known Route 66. At that time, there were no Arizona communities of any size further north.

Route 66
Today, Interstate 40 bisects northern Arizona, carrying cross-country travelers to and from Southern California in multiple lanes at 70 to 80 miles per hour.
In 1950, those travelers instead got "their kicks on Route 66" which, far more slowly and much more dangerously, carried traffic in two lanes between Chicago and Santa Monica. Bisecting Northern Arizona, each day the fabled roadway carried thousands of motorists en route to tourist attractions in Arizona and the orchards and beaches of southern California. In those days the lure of Los Angeles included Hollywood and Knott's Berry Farm, but not yet Disneyland. Route 66 was perhaps the most-traveled two lanes of blacktop in the world -- and certainly the most famous.
From the time those making this southwesterly passage entered Arizona south of Fort Defiance, in addition to parades of signs bearing Burma-Shave limericks, they encountered a constant

stream of roadside billboards and come-ons enticing them to visit real and exaggerated roadside attractions.

Some, such as the Painted Desert and Petrified Forest were world-class stops, as were Monument Valley and the Grand Canyon to the north and Meteor Crater to the south.

Monument Valley, with its spectacular rock spires and vistas, had been the setting for many movies involving such notables as John Wayne, Glenn Ford and Alan Ladd. However, because it was several hours north, most of those traveling Route 66 missed it.

Meteor Crater, located a few miles south, was also less frequently visited than the Grand Canyon and other northern Arizona attractions. It is a massive, mile-wide impact crater -- a place where astronauts trained -- but once at its rim there was little to do but turn around and leave. The thrill of looking at a huge hole -- even one of the world's largest -- has its limitations.

Of more interest were the Hopis and Navajos through whose reservations Route 66 passed, and their blankets, pottery, and silver and turquoise jewelry that could be purchased at trading posts and roadside stands.

Flagstaff

Alongside the main east-west line of the Atchison, Topeka and Santa Fe railway with Harvey Houses and uniformed Harvey Girls at its major southwestern stops, Flagstaff was the primary gateway to the Grand Canyon and Monument Valley.

<u>Thursday, December 28, 1950</u>

Miami   101
Flagstaff 28

Playing at home with each player scoring, Miami topped 100 points and won by 73. Acevedo led the Vandals with 28 points. Trujillo followed with 20. Lazovich had 19.

Winslow
Winslow (noted in song by the Eagles for "standing on the corner watching the girls go by") is located east of Flagstaff between Meteor Crater and the Petrified Forest / Painted Desert.

Friday, December 29, 1950
Miami 79 Winslow 32

Playing at home, with every player scoring, Lazovich scored 22 points. Trujillo added 21. Coming off the bench, Elias Delgadillo scored 10. Miami won by 37 points.

Week Five:

Duncan
Located (with Clifton and Morenci) in Greenlee County four miles west of the New Mexico border, Duncan is a small community that straddles the Gila River. The nation's first woman Justice of the Supreme Court, Sandra Day O'Connor, grew up on the nearby Lazy J Ranch. In 1954, Duncan played in the finals of the State Class B Tournament, losing 47-39 to Phoenix Carver.

Playing at home, Miami defeated Duncan's 4-3 Wildcats by 56 points. Miami was led by Lazovich with 26 points. Trujillo added 17 and Acevedo 15.

Friday, January 5, 1951

Miami   94
Duncan   38

Safford

Located on Highway 70 en route to North Carolina via Lordsburg, New Mexico, Safford is 77 miles east of Globe (in 1951 several miles more because of a then winding, circuitous route around and across Coolidge Dam).

Situated on the Gila River, it was then primarily a farming community, but copper has since become a major industry.

Safford sits at the foot of 10,720-foot Mt. Graham in the Pinaleno Mountains, one of central and southern Arizona's "sky islands." It is home to Mt. Graham International Observatory, which has one of the world's largest and most powerful binocular telescopes.

Former U.S. Football League quarterback Fred Mortensen, who played at ASU, is a Safford native.

Saturday, January 6, 1951

Miami   94
Safford 50

Fito Trujillo, the smallest player on the Miami team, set a state scoring record with 45 points, despite fouling out with more than 2 1/2 minutes to play. The Silver Belt proclaimed that the 135-pound guard's performance had made him "one of Arizona's all-time basketball greats." At the time he fouled out, Fito's point total exceeded that of the entire Safford team. He missed just one field goal and two free throws. Eli Lazovich scored 14.

Week Six:

> ### Clifton and U.S. 666
>
> Located on then U.S. 666 ("The Coronado Trail"), Clifton is a historic copper mining community near the New Mexico border.
>
> Geronimo, the notorious Apache leader, was reportedly born nearby.
>
> The Federal Highway Administration's on-line Highway History states that U.S. 666 became the object of controversy because in the Bible "666" is the "number of the beast" (antichrist). That earned it the nickname "Devil's Highway." It was reportedly featured in a Lions Gate Home Entertainment movie titled *Route 666*, staring Lou Diamond Phillips, and briefly in director Oliver Stone's *Natural Born Killers*.
>
> Citing Jonathan D. Rosenblum's history of a 1983-86 strike by the United Steelworkers of America against the Phelps Dodge copper company (*Copper Crucible*, Cornell University Press, Second Edition, 1998), the on-line Highway History states:
>
>> Route 666 rides the rugged eastern seam of Arizona from the Petrified Forest, south, across the Zuni River, through the Apache National Forest, and into the mountain mining towns of Clifton and Morenci. Unlike the straightforward, gentle passage of retired Route 66 ("America's Highway"), U.S. 666, its descendant, is tortuous, wild, and as strange as its name. In little more than one hundred miles, the surrounding altitude ranges from twenty-nine

hundred feet to more than eleven thousand feet. With some four hundred twisting curves in one sixty-mile stretch, the road has sent more than its share of travelers crashing off cliffs. If, as Nat King Cole sang, drivers get their kicks on Route 66, they take their risks on 666.

He was quoted as having stated that people living along the road "worried over a possible connection between ancient symbolism and their modern fate."

In 2003, the highway was re-numbered 491.

<u>Friday, January 12, 1951</u>

Miami   122
Clifton   58

Playing at home, Globe's archrival scored 122 points against a highly regarded 9-1 Clifton team. Eli Lazovich set a state scoring record with 50 points, breaking the record of 45 Trujillo set just a week before.

The 122 points was also a state record. It broke Miami's own record of 103 set in 1948 during Coach Kivisto's first year as Miami's coach.

The Silver Belt reported that Miami led by just one point, 19 to 18, at the end of the first quarter. Miami won by 64 points.

In addition to Lazovich's 50, Acevedo scored 30. Miami's Hector Jacott held Clifton's leading scorer to just four points.

The Silver Belt observed: "If there was ever any doubt that the Vandal basketball squad is one of the best cage quintets ever to play on an Arizona court, it was dispelled Friday night."

In nearby Globe, the January night was chilly. At the Tiger's Friday night post-game dance, students were slow dancing to the music of Miami's Sanchez brothers and their theme song "Tencia (I Love You So)," written by a band member for his Globe girlfriend. Like a sudden chill breeze, the news from Miami swept through the auditorium.

Pima

Founded by Mormon settlers just a few miles west of Thatcher and Safford, Pima is located on Highway 70 along the Gila River. Originating in New Mexico and providing irrigation water en route, the Gila River flows east to west for 649 miles, across the entire state of Arizona. before merging with the Colorado River at Yuma on the California border.

Saturday, January 13, 1951

Miami   56
Pima   28

Although losing by 28 points, playing at home the 5-2 Roughriders checked Miami's high scoring. The Silver Belt reported:

> To keep possession of the ball, Pima refused to take 19 free throws, preferring instead to take it out of bounds .... Time after time they maneuvered into scoring position, only to pass the ball back out and continue stalling. [34]

The Silver Belt noted that "at the end of the game, Pima fans

---

[34] At that time, a team could choose whether to shoot its free throws or instead take the ball out of bounds.

cheered their coach as if he had won...."

Lazovich scored 15 points. Acevedo added 14, and Trujillo 12.

Looking ahead to another slow-down game in next week's return encounter at Miami, the Silver Belt noted that "Pima holds a definite height superiority" with a starting lineup averaging nearly 6'3".

Week Seven:

A week later at Miami, Pima's height advantage and slow-down game was not nearly as effective. Miami won by 59 points.

Friday, January 19, 1951

Miami   80
Pima   21

Acevedo led the Vandals with 22 points. Lazovich had 21.

Again, Fort Thomas forfeited.

Saturday, February 10, 1950

Miami   Wins Forfeit
Fort Thomas   Loses Forfeit

Week Eight:

Miami played three games in week eight.

Morenci

Located just a few miles "up-mountain" from Clifton, Morenci was a "company town." Currently, Morenci's biggest employer (and that of nearby Clifton) is Freeport-McMoRan. With a massive open pit, its Morenci Mine is the largest copper mining operation in North America, and one of the largest in the world.

Collapsed Church on Eagle Creek near Morenci

<u>Thursday, January 25, 1951</u>

Miami   77
Morenci   44

At Morenci, the Wildcats held Miami to a 33-point victory margin. Led by Lazovich's 24 points, all of the Miami players scored.

<u>Friday, January 26, 1951</u>

Miami   92
Clifton   72

At Clifton the following night, the Vandals won by just 20 points. Trujillo scored 40.

> Saturday, January 27, 1951
>
> Miami   99
> Duncan   47

At Duncan, Lupe Acevedo scored 56 points -- becoming the third Vandal to break the state scoring record in four weeks. The Silver Belt reported:

> Duncan fans themselves got carried away by Acevedo's deadly accuracy. Toward the end of the game they were shouting "Two points!" just as soon as the ball left his hands headed for the basket. Their confidence wasn't wasted …. Out of 24 shots …, Lupe sank 22 …. He showed equal adeptness on the free-throw line making 12 out of 14 tries….

The Vandals won by 52 points.

Week Nine:

Regarding the upcoming weekend games, the Silver Belt reported:

> With the sporting eyes of the entire state watching their unstoppable brand of play, the Vandals leave home again this weekend for what will almost certainly be their 54th and 55th consecutive conference wins in Thatcher and Safford.
>
> Both teams have previously been handed stinging defeats by Miami's talent-laden crew….

Coach Kivisto is expected to substitute freely during both games to give his reserves valuable game practice. It is interesting to note that Miami carries a varsity squad of 10 men and usually plays all of them in the course of a game....

<u>Friday, February 2, 1951</u>

Miami   57
Thatcher 39

The Silver Belt reported: "The Eagles refused to take 21 free throws to take the ball out of bounds...." Acevedo scored 24 points, with Trujillo scoring just eight and Lazovich only four.

<u>Saturday, February 3, 1951</u>

Miami   72
Safford 43

Miami led 43 to 18 at the half and, according to the Silver Belt "Coach Kivisto used his reserves for a good portion of the tilt...." Lazovich led all scorers with 22. The Silver Belt added:

> Seeing that his boys are tiring a little under the heavy strain of their jet-propelled style of play, Coach Ernie Kivisto is giving them a well-deserved rest this week....

That week, W. Jay Burk, a sports columnist for the Arizona Republic in Phoenix wrote:

> Miami High School may have the greatest natural high school team in the country. There are a lot of high school mentors out in the Eastern Conference who believe the Vandals can whip any Arizona school,

A or B, by 20 points or more. Be that as it may, Coach Ernie Kivisto has a powerhouse and one we'd like to see in action.

There are a lot of March of Dimes games around right now. Is it too late to hook up the Kivisto Kids in a Phoenix benefit -- say against Phoenix Union? That game should pack the roomy quarters of the P.U. gym to the rafters.

Phoenix is the center of population in Arizona and it would be fitting to bring one of the country's greatest prep scoring machines here for all to see. Certainly boys like Lupe Acevedo, Eli Lazovich, and Fito Trujillo deserve to have their wares paraded in the brightest limelight.
....
The Aladdin who may rub the magic lamp of his own ingenuity to bring out a defensive genie capable of stopping the mad march of Miami is J.S. (Joe) Flipper of Carver High. Whether or not Carver will get to meet the Vandals in the Class B tourney at Tucson remains to be seen. However, Coach Flipper has solved other attacks before, and has a good sound ball club with which to do the trick. His own associates in the coaching business think that this protégé of Kansas U. and Phog Allen is the tops.

Week Ten:

Friday, February 9, 1951
Miami   130
Morenci   43

Playing at home in a game the author saw, the Vandals set a national scoring record. The Silver Belt reported:

> Fans gasped in amazement as the Vandals put shot after shot from every angle and distance through the hoop, with hardly a miss. The inspired squad was the answer to a basketball coach's dream as it made 78.8 per cent of it's tries at the basket….
>
> It was team work … rather than any individual player that broke the national scoring record. Superb ball-handling and close co-operation dazzled the Tigers [Wildcats] and set up scoring opportunities in rapid succession….
>
> Morenci, reeling under the staggering blows of the lightning-fast Vandals, was all but powerless. In a futile attempt to put a lid on the scoring, they tried a trick now familiar to the feared Miami aggregation -- they stalled as much as possible. To keep possession, they declined 16 out of 21 free throws to take the ball out of bounds instead.
>
> [T]he Vandal second string team … swished 25 points in the last four minutes.

Acevedo led the Vandals with 38 points, followed by Lazovich with 30, Trujillo with 20. Al Lobato scored 20 off the bench; and Rudy Moreno had 10.

Observing that "two years ago, the Vandals … set a national average of 70.1 points a game," the Silver Belt noted several of the Vandals' achievements to date. They included:

- scoring an average of 84 points a game, with the national high school average being only about 42 points a game;

- compiling that average in 32-minute games and, by comparison, the "highest professional scoring average, made in games 60 minutes long, is 82.7, held by the Minneapolis [now Los Angeles] Lakers;"

- having taken only one time out all year, to their opponents 86; and

- having taken only 11 timeouts during the past four years to their opponents 396.

The Silver Belt added:

> According to Jim Cordy, Associated Press sports editor in New York who telephoned Coach Kivisto when he heard about Miami's record-smashing, the Vandal cager's fistful of honors is absolutely tops.
>
> Mr. Cordy asked for every scrap of information available on the team, plus pictures. It looks as though Miami will soon be better known for basketball than for copper.

The Arizona Republic reported:

> Miami High's all-conquering Vandals -- Arizona's only unbeaten prep basketball quint -- shattered what is believed to be the national high school single-game scoring record ... by drubbing Morenci 130 to 43.
>
> Miami's total eclipsed the record of 125 set in 1946 by Muncie, Ind. High.

Every member of Miami's 10-man squad broke into the scoring column as the Vandals racked up their 50th consecutive home court triumph and their 56th straight Eastern Conference victory.

In Other News

Also, that day the Republic reported:

- As a junior, Bisbee, Arizona's Hadley Hicks had received high school All-American honorable mention;[35] and

- Joe DiMaggio had joined Babe Ruth as the only baseball players to have been paid $l million over the course of a career. The INS release noted:

    > The million-buck club now includes Babe Ruth and Joe DiMaggio in baseball; Joe Louis, Jack Dempsey and Gene Tunney in boxing; Walter Hagen in golf; and jockeys Eddie Arcaro, Johnny Longden and Ted Atkinson on the turf....

    It added:

    > Baseball has two others -- Ted Williams of the Red Sox and Bob Feller of the Indians -- who may join the club before they hang up their spikes.

---

[35] A year later, Hicks was named to the 1951-1952 All American High School Football and Track teams. Bisbee retired his No. 20 football jersey when he graduated. He was the Governor of Arizona Boys State in 1951, served in the United States Army from 1954 to 1956, and earned a bachelor's degree in Education from Arizona State University, where he also played baseball. He later earned a master's degree from the University of Montana and served on the board of the Arizona Athletic Hall of Fame.

Week Eleven:

On Sunday, February 11, W. Jay Burk wrote for the Arizona Republic:

> The most controversial subject in the state today is Miami basketball. The 2½ points-per minute Vandals are the greatest group of school boy scorers in the nation and the news services blazed that fact to every point of the compass following Friday's 130-43 debacle over Morenci....
>
> Skeptics and boosters alike are agreed on one point. The Class B tournament in Tucson is going to prove Ernie Kivisto's Vandals a really sensational basketball aggregation, or stamp them as just another good team that belabored the buckets out of weak opposition.
>
> While on the subject of the Class B classic in Old Pueblo, we will pass along a little comment that has come from several sources. It is to do with seeding the strong arrays, so that all the best clubs aren't in the same bracket.... [I]t was of state-wide interest last season when four tough district champs, Miami, Nogales, Florence, and Carver, were all grouped in the lower bracket....
>
> One other Miami matter.... [A] staunch Miami booster believes that the meeting between Miami and Phoenix Union Coyotes, Class A's almost certain champs, could be brought about by a pressure of public opinion....
>
> Such a game would have to be a quickie. In our first effort here following Ray Silvius' departure to jet-

jockeying for Uncle Sam, we suggested such a battle....

The Coyotes ... are willing to take on Miami and vice-versa. However, the only avenue open was for one opponent on each schedule forfeiting so that the Pack and the kiting-Kivistans could collide. No post-season games are allowed by the AIA, and only 20 games, prior to tourney-play, are allowed any one club.

Several angles were attempted but there were too many dead-end turns ..., so we'll have to catch a glimpse of Miami on some other court, as will the rest of the Phoenix fans.

In Other News

- The Arizona Republic carried an INS release by Pat Robinson under the banner "Scribe Says Fan Shouldn't Pay to Watch Female Athletes." From New York, Mr. Robinson wrote:

  > [W]e think it is an imposition to ask the public to pay to watch female athletes in action.
  >
  > There is no game which men do not play better and, with us at least, no amount of lace-edged silk panties is ever going to compensate for their lack of skill.
  >
  > In our eyes the gals lose their grace, charm and femininity when they parade their lack of athletic skill ....
  >
  > Take the AAU indoor championships the other day

as a case in point. Skinny gals, fat gals, bow-legged and knock-kneed gals were cluttering up the place to our utmost disgust.

- The Republic reported that Sugar Ray Robinson, the welterweight champion of the world, had taken the middle-weight title from Jake ("Raging Bull") LaMotta by a TKO in the 13th round.

- Class A St. Mary's, which Class B Nogales defeated on its early season trip to Phoenix, shocked Phoenix Union 49-27 on the Coyotes home court in what the Republic termed "the greatest high school upset of the season."

Up next were home and away games against arch-rival Globe.

<u>Friday, February 16, 1951</u> (at Miami)
Miami 105 Globe 61

Led by Acevedo's 28 points, with strong support from Lazovich and Trujillo, each with 24, and Rudy Moreno with 15, the Vandals outscored rival Globe by 44 points. This was Miami's last game in the gymnasium it had used since 1922.

<u>Saturday, February 17, 1951</u> (at Globe)
Miami 102 Globe 49

Published weekly, the Silver Belt reported the following Thursday that for Globe "forward [George] Daves was high in the series, hitting for 18 points Friday night."[36] It added:

> Miami's record-smashing cage squad put the lid on the first undefeated basketball season in the high school's history last weekend by delivering two crushing defeats to a game Globe five, 104 to 62 and 102 to 49.
>
> The victories cinched Miami's fourth consecutive Eastern Conference championship and made the Vandals the only undefeated team in the entire state.
>
> The ever-present rivalry between Miami and Globe brought some rough, hard playing into both conflicts …. Emily Post Etiquette was occasionally forgotten….
>
> The century mark was reached both times largely through the deadly accuracy of Miami's famed Three Horsemen -- Lupe Acevedo, Eli Lazovich and Fito Trujillo. Friday night's tussle saw them get 28, 24, and 24, respectively, to account for 76 of the 105 points.
>
> Acevedo's havoc at the hoop was spoiled somewhat

---

[36] Fifteen years later another member of that Globe team, Air Force Captain Jack Tomes was shot down over North Vietnam. He spent 6 ½ years as a captive of the North Vietnamese. Part of that was at the infamous "Hanoi Hilton." He was joined there for 5 ½ years by his Globe team-mate, Air Force Captain Charles Tyler. Captain Tomes was the starting half-back on the Globe football team on which Captain Tyler was the starting tackle. Reportedly, one Christmas Eve, Jack's baritone voice broke the night silence with a rendition of "Silent Night;" after which he was severely punished and almost died. Yet, the following year he reportedly sang it again – this time joined by others; and the rules were changed to permit the annual singing of a hymn. Following his release, Jack retired from the Air Force as a Colonel. Also as a Colonel, Charles Tyler returned to active duty.

the following evening when Globe put two or three men on him to put an almost score-tight fence around him. The other two-thirds of the trio compensated, however, with Lazovich swishing a solid 30 points and Trujillo close behind with 28.

The hoop marksmen made 64.4 per cent of their shots good Friday night and moved over to the Globe court to sink a torrid 76.2 per cent Saturday evening….

Regular Season Recap
20 wins - 0 losses (22-0 with forfeits)
Average Points Per Game:
Miami   85.9
Opponents 42.9
Average Victory Margin: 43

With the regular season over and the Eastern Conference tournament about to begin, titled *"Secret of Vandal Cage Success Revealed,"* Philip A. Waggener wrote in the Silver Belt:

> Ending the season in a scoring blaze of glory, the Miami High School's cage quintet proved itself to be one of the outstanding prep teams in the nation.
>
> The Vandals scorched a blistering path through all of their opposition to end up with a fistful of honors which has never been even approached heretofore by any high school basketball team anywhere.
>
> The question which immediately rises in most people's minds is: How did they do it? How could a small-town team playing against formidable opponents, be so white-hot?

The answer lies in two things -- talent and condition.

Once in a coach's lifetime (if he's lucky) does there ever come up a team so loaded with superb talent as the present Vandal crew. Lupe Acevedo, Eli Lazovich, Fito Trujillo -- each of them is worthy of having a team built around himself. And even without these three, Miami would probably boast a Conference-winning squad, with Al Lobato, Rudy Moreno, Hector Jacott, Leigh Larson, Elias Delgadillo, Andy Rumic and Dick Vargas all exhibiting top-caliber playing ability.

But talent alone would not put the Vandals at the top of the basketball world. An equally important factor is that every player has been honed to the keen edge of perfect physical condition and kept that way by Coach Ernie Kivisto.
....
Opponents who try to match the Vandals' jet-propelled brand of play find themselves completely exhausted after a very few moments of play. A glance at the statistics will verify this. During the season just ended, Miami's opponents have taken a total of 96 time outs, while the Vandals themselves have taken just one!

Probably no other high school team in the country devotes itself so completely to basketball as does the Miami quintet. Starting with the first pre-season practice session the team members are on a strict schedule ....

The first week of practice is rough. The boys go home with aching leg muscles and blistered feet. After that, it gets easier, but there is still no let-up. Every night during the season from 4 to 6:30, they run through scrimmages and calisthenics that would make you tired just to watch. A dynamic, restless man himself, Coach Kivisto keeps his boys moving and moving fast for the entire 2½ hours.

Rough on the boys, you say? Perhaps in one sense yes, but remember, they are all doing it voluntarily and for the love of basketball ….

And it has been a valuable asset to the boys, too. They have experienced the rare "espirit de corps" of being part of a harmonious, invincible team. Getting down to more tangible things, they have received scores of offers for scholarships from many of the top universities in the nation.

Right after Saturday night's Globe game, Rev. John Dodu, dean of men at Loyola University, asked the six top players to come to Loyola under liberal scholarships.

The Eastern Conference Tournament

In the News:

- Monday's Arizona Republic led the week with a startling front-page headline: "CCNY Charged With 'Throwing' Arizona Game." By-lined New York, the article read:

    The City College of New York basketball loss to the University of Arizona in Madison Square Garden Dec. 28 was a "fixed" game in which the losing players each collected $1,000 from gamblers, it was charged here Sunday in the latest of a series of basketball gambling episodes in the East.

    Players at City College, New York University, and a former Long Island University player are involved in Sunday's charges ….

    The latest scandal exploded within a month of the Manhattan College "fix" expose ….

    The district attorney said the players told him they had not agreed to lose, but had agreed to see that the "spread" or margin of victory would not be more than three points.

- Also, on the front page, the Republic reported: "China Reds Driven Back 6 Miles East of Seoul."

- In other news that day, on the sports page, the Republic:

    ➢ reported that 38-year-old Woody Hayes had been named football coach at Ohio State.

> reported that "Stan Musial signed his 1951 contract with the St. Louis Cardinals Sunday for a salary which the club owner ... said 'probably is higher than that paid any other player in either league." Musial had "wanted $100,000 for 1951 but ... might be getting more than that." The Cardinals' owner "explained he used the word 'probably' because he didn't know the exact amount given Ted Williams. The Red Sox slugger reportedly got $125,000 last year and signed for the same figure this year."

> promoted an upcoming event at Phoenix Country Club with a photo of Joe DiMaggio golfing with brother Dominic, a Red Sox outfielder.

- On Wednesday, the Republic published an AP report titled "1951 'Black Sox' Cage Scandal Matches 1919 Debacle." It read in part:

    Nineteen fifty-one will go down in history as the year of the infamous 'Black Sox' scandal in basketball.

    Nothing in sport – except the dirty gambling web that enmeshed Shoeless Joe Jackson, Eddie Cicotte, and other baseball greats of the 1919 Chicago-Cincinnati World Series – has matched the scope of the present game-fixing expose.

    The top teams in the nation and some of the best of the modern players are involved....
    ....
    Three stars of the sophomore [City College of New York] "Cinderella Team" that won basketball's only "grand slam" – the [National]

Invitational and the NCAA – in 1950 admitted they accepted bribes to fix three CCNY games this year – Missouri, Arizona and Boston College.

Week Twelve:

Thursday, February 22, 1951 (First Round)
Miami 88
Safford 30

Played at Globe, Miami opened the Eastern Conference tournament with a tournament record 88 points, defeating Safford by 58 points. Eli Lazovich scored a tournament record 30 points -- equal to Safford's entire output -- followed by Acevedo with 22.

In Other News:

From a Columbia, South Carolina AP report in the Republic:

> The state senate Thursday concurred in a house resolution asking the reinstatement in organized baseball of 'Shoeless Joe' Jackson.
>
> The resolution will be sent to A.B. Chandler, baseball commissioner, and presidents of the American and National Leagues.
>
> Jackson, who lives at Greenville, S.C. was thrown out of baseball after the 1919 World Series 'Black Sox' scandal. He was an outfielder with the Chicago White Sox.

> Friday, February 23, 1951 (Semi-Finals)
>
> Miami 95
> Globe 49

Bannered "Miami Cracks More Records," the Republic reported:

> Miami broke its own tournament record in the Globe tourney by whipping Globe, 95 to 49. Eli Lazovich also broke his tourney single game mark by slipping in 33 points for the winners, who also are favored in the state tournament. Fito Trujillo added 17, Lupe Acevedo 15, for the Vandals, who worked up a 53-24 halftime lead. They won their 22nd game of an unbeaten season and their 60th straight conference victory.

A separate Republic article reported:

> In Phoenix, Ajo and Carver, heavy favorites, advanced to the round of two in the West Central. At Chandler, Casa Grande and Chandler pulled off a pair of upsets to gain East Central finals. In Bisbee, Nogales and Willcox pulled safely into the finals of the Southern Conference and at Globe, Miami and Pima survived in Eastern play.

> Saturday, February 24, 1951 (Finals)
> Miami 57
> Pima 42

The Republic reported:

> Coach Ernie Kivisto's hot hoopsters were given quite a tussle by the valiant Pima Roughriders before

winning 57-42.

The rangy Miamians started fast and kept control all the way, but were outplayed on the floor by the losers. Pima, however, lacked the bright-eyed marksmanship of Miami, who were led by Eli Lazovich and Lupe Acevedo, each getting 14….

The score at the end of the first period was 19-8, and 29-17 at halftime. The third period closed at 46-28.

The Silver Belt reported on the game as follows:

[T]he Vandals bogged down both offensively and defensively against the Roughriders to emerge with a narrow 57-42 win….

[T]he Vandals did not come near their usual court perfection. Less than 20 per cent of their tries at the hoop were good, and their ball-handling lacked its usual dazzling accuracy.

The Republic also reported:

- "Phoenix Union Captures City Crown 54-49."

- "Carver Jolts Ajo for West Central Meet Title."

- "Casa Grande Snares East Central Diadem," adding: "The Casa Grande Cougars, mythical state Class B football champions, added the East Central district basketball title here Saturday night with a 27-24 victory over Chandler in the finals."

- "Nogales Cops Southern Title."

In Other News:

A United Press release from Kansas City reported:

> Coach Forrest C. ("Phog") Allen of Kansas University charged Friday that danger of another major basketball scandal lurks in Kansas City's Municipal Auditorium.
>
> Allen, in a written statement said, "It is a well known and accepted fact that there is a certain gang of gamblers and bookmakers that control odds in Kansas City. They are to be found in the same box in Municipal Auditorium at every basketball game I've ever attended there...."

Conference Tournament Recap

Miami   3 wins / 0 losses
Average Points Per Game:
Miami   80.0
Opponents   40.4
Average Victory Margin: 39.6
Season to date: 23 - 0

The State Tournament

Headlined "Phoenix Union, Miami State Prep Title Choices," on Monday, February 26th the Republic reported that drawings for the state Class B tourney had been completed and "two district winners fell into both the upper and lower brackets."

The Silver Belt reported:

> Heavily favored to win the state championship, the Vandals are rated as the most potent team in the tourney.
>
> A big question mark was thrown over Miami's chances, however, by their sudden let-down in the last game of the Eastern conference Tournament last weekend against Pima. A similar let-down in the state tourney would almost certainly mean elimination.
>
> Most fans, however, are of the opinion that the near-catastrophe Saturday night was just what the Vandals needed to put them on their toes for the Tucson tilts.
>
> Coach Ernie Kivisto put his boys through what he termed 'the roughest workouts they have ever had' Monday and Tuesday. The boys didn't need any prodding, however. They knew they slacked off Saturday and were out to make up for it.

Tuesday, February 27th, brought stunning news. Topping the Republic's sports page was the headline: "Coyotes Stripped of Class-A Cage Crown." The article read:

> Phoenix Union Monday was stripped of its Class A

championship when it was discovered an ineligible player had played in or suited up for 12 games.

Phoenix Union officials had discovered that Carlos Holland, substitute forward who had played but 43 minutes in games already won and who had but 11 points all season, was 20 instead of 18 as he had indicated….

On Wednesday, captioned "Fans Eager To See Miami High's Cagers," the Republic carried an AP release from Tucson that read:

More than ordinary interest is being taken in the Class B high school basketball tourney which starts at the University of Arizona Thursday morning because of the high scoring record of the Miami Vandals.

Miami has attracted a certain amount of national attention by scoring more than 100 points in several of its games.

More than one college coach is expected to drop into the Arizona gym while the Vandals are in action. Several of the boys are considered splendid college prospects.

On Thursday, the Republic carried twin banners: "Phoenix Union No. 1 Choice on ASC Court" and "Miami Heavy Favorite in Class B Meet." The articles read:

Phoenix Union, stripped of its season championship by loss of 12 games in which an ineligible player figured, still is seeded No. 1 … and rates that position because of a 17-1 season record….

Miami was established as the heavy favorite on the eve of the Class B state championship basketball tournament Wednesday. Carver and Nogales are rated as the chief threats to the blazing Vandals, who have slashed their way to 23 triumphs without defeat this year and who have spearheaded the Eastern Conference for the past three years.

Included in the Vandal victory string is a defeat of Nogales, one of its chief threats. That was accomplished at Nogales, a feat all the more impressive. Carver and Nogales fought to [a] standstill in Phoenix, the Apaches gaining a one-point decision early in the season before the Monarchs gained momentum.

In Other News:

In the Republic sports section that week:

- From the AP in New York: "Ninth Player Arrested In Basketball Scandal."

- In "Good Sports" by "Edge," the inimitable caricaturist Kearney Egerton profiled Casey Stengal. With his hallmark sketches, the text included:

    > His world champion New York Yankees are tuning up for the defense of their American League pennant and World Series crown in spring drills at Phoenix Municipal Stadium.

- "Yanks Will Look Long At McDougald" and "Mantle, Carey Also To Have Studied Trial." The article stated:

[Manager Casey Stengal] has decided that Gil McDougald, the second baseman who was most valuable player in the Texas League last year for Beaumont, will be used at third base from now on. "We'll see if he can learn to play it," Stengal said Monday. "Maybe he can make the club."

Stengal's thinking was along the lines that even if he moved his varsity second baseman, Jerry Coleman to third, a position he knows well and where he would give the Yanks a solid left side of the infield, it would break up the double play combination that led the American League last year. Coleman teamed with Phil Rizzuto at shortstop in executing the twin killings….

… [I]t was also considered probable that McDougald, Mickey Mantle, shortstop last year with Joplin, who also will get in some time at third base from now on, Andy Carey, the third baseman signed off the St. Mary's College campus, and three or four of the farmhand pitchers would be held over for longer looks.

"We'll try Mantle at third a while," said Stengal, "and see how he does. Later, we'll decide whether he's a shortstop, third baseman, or outfielder."

A decision is also pending on Bill Skowron, the third baseman from Purdue. "I've heard he can play right field," a somewhat surprised Stengal remarked. "Maybe he's better there than left field. We have too many third basemen already."

On Wednesday, the Republic sports section featured a photo of Yogi Berra, "the Yankee catcher who is holding out for a reputed $40,000. ..."

The Republic's entertainment fare included advertisements for:

- Mae West's upcoming "in person" stage appearance as "*Diamond Lil*" at the Paramount;

- "*Cry Danger*" with Dick Powell and Rhonda Fleming at the Fox;

- "*The Great Manhunt*" with Douglas Fairbanks, Jr., at the Palms;

- "*King Solomon's Mines*" with Deborah Kerr and Stewart Granger and "*Lady Without a Passport*" with Hedy Lamarr at the Rialto;

- "*Branded*" with Alan Ladd at the Aero;

- "*Mark of Zorro*" with Tyrone Power at the Ramona;

- "*The Blazing Sun*" with Gene Autry and Champion "*World's Wonder Horse*" at the Strand;

- Rudyard Kipling's "*Kim*" with Errol Flynn, Van Johnson and Kathryn Grayson at the New Mesa;

- "The Savage Charm ... the Stormy Life ... the Many Loves" of "*Valentino*" at the Paramount;

- "*All About Eve*" with Bette Davis, Anne Baxter and Celeste Holm at the Pioneer Drive-In;

- *"So Proudly We Hail"* with Claudette Colbert and Paulette Goddard and *"Beau Geste"* with Gary Cooper and Ray Milland at the Drive-In; and

- *"Atrocities of Manila"* at the Vista.[37]

Week Thirteen:

Miami's first state tournament opponent was Holbrook.

Holbrook
Like season opponents Flagstaff and Winslow, Holbrook was also on Route 66. It is the county seat of Navajo County and the gateway to the Petrified Forest and Painted Desert. Milwaukee Bucks coach Mike Budenholzer grew up in Holbrook. The Bucks defeated the Phoenix Suns for the 2021 NBA championship.
Located on what was once the Atlantic and Pacific Railroad, Holbrook became the headquarters for the Aztec Land and Cattle Company (the fabled "Hashknife Outfit"). In the late 1800s the Hashknife Outfit owned or leased two million acres and was one of

---

[37] Pandering to still fresh images and reports of World War II savagery and atrocities by Japanese soldiers, the ad trumpeted the movie as for "Adults Only" -- "An Unbelievable, Shocking True Thriller" -- "See ... Captive Women Tortured!" "Cruel! Barbaric! Vicious!" "Raping Murderers Satisfying Their Lust!" Contrary to that stereotype, Bill Kajikawa, a Japanese American who with the author's mother attended Phoenix Union High School in the early-1930s, was highly regarded by all who knew him. A superior athlete, he became a revered coach at ASC-Tempe (ASU) and is a member of ASU's Hall of Distinction. During World War II he served with the Army's 442nd Regimental Combat Team. Comprised of Japanese Americans, it has been termed the Army's most decorated combat unit. His daughter, Christine Kajikawa Wilkinson, became Senior Vice-President and Secretary of ASU and served as its interim Athletic Director three times.

the largest cattle ranches ever. Many Hashknife cowboys were wanted men hiding from the law. Rustling of Hashknife cattle and horses was common; and the Hashknife played a role in the 1880's Pleasant Valley War.

The Navajo County Historical Society describes Holbrook at that time as follows:

> During the 1880s, Holbrook developed into one of the toughest and most lawless towns in the country. According to one source, in a period of one year, twenty-six gun victims were planted in Holbrook's graveyard. Shooting brawls usually broke up dances and public gatherings, and at least several times each week drunken cowboys or badmen galloped their horses through town, firing their six-shooters, shattering store windows and wounding bystanders who were too slow to take cover.
>
> Not only was the town being ravaged by outlaws, but by 1886 this lawless element was also running wild in the surrounding countryside. A bitter cattle-sheep war was in progress to the southeast of Holbrook; a small scale war, between the Graham and Tewksbury factions, was raging in Pleasant Valley in Tonto Basin to the south of Holbrook; and a wholesale rustlers' campaign was in full swing on the cattle range near Holbrook. Many outlaws chased out of Texas by the Rangers came to the Holbrook area and hired out to the Hashknife Outfit under an assumed name.
>
> Possibly the most famous man in Holbrook's colorful past was Commodore Perry Owens, newly elected Apache County Sheriff [before Navajo County existed] and a principal of the town's best-known gun battle....

He wore twin forty-fives at his hips and carried a Winchester repeater in his saddle scabbard.... Holbrook became a peaceful town after the Blevins fight, with only an occasional killing to break the monotony.

With a mustache and long, dark hair flowing onto his chest, Owens was famously photographed holding the barrel of a rifle pointed upward from the floor, a pistol holstered backward on his left hip, and two ammunition belts around his waist (one for the rifle; one for the pistol) – not the look of a man to be trifled with. The Argus in Holbrook described him as "a quiet, unassuming person, strictly honorable and upright in his dealings with all men and enjoyed the respect and confidence of all who knew him."

Regarding the Blevins/Cooper shootout, a source states:

> In 1887 Sheriff Owens sought to arrest Andy Blevins (aka Andy Cooper) for horse theft. The Blevins, including Cooper, were allied with the Graham faction in the Pleasant Valley War and Cooper had bragged of and was thought to have been responsible for multiple killings, including one of the Tewksburys and a companion who had been recently ambushed in Pleasant Valley. Precipitating one of the west's most dangerous and deadly shootouts, Sheriff Owens went alone to the Blevins' Holbrook house. Unlike the *High Noon* showdown when promised assistance of townsfolk disappeared, saying "I don't want anyone hurt," Sheriff Owens refused assistance. Exposed in the open outside the Blevins' house, Owens shot Cooper,

> two brothers and a friend; and all but one brother died. Owens was unhurt. His bravery rivaled that of the legendary Earp brothers and Doc Holiday at Tombstone's OK Corral.

> Thursday, March 1, 1951 (First Round)
>
> Miami   96
> Holbrook 70

The Republic trumpeted: "Carver Triumphs, Miami Mauls Foe," stating: "Three Miami players scored more points than the entire Holbrook team." Lupe Acevedo had 34, Eli Lazovich 27, and Fito Trujillo 18.

Elsewhere in the Arizona Republic:

- At Montgomery Ward men's sharkskin suits were $29.75.
- Headlined "Duke Cager Shatters Scoring Records," from New York the AP reported:

> The National Collegiate Athletic Bureau said Thursday [Dick] Groat had established a scoring high for one season when he boosted his 1950-51 total to 746 points. He hit the mark in Duke's final regular game…

Groat averaged 25 points a game that year.

Miami's next opponent was Scottsdale.

> **Scottsdale**
>
> Then a much smaller suburb of Phoenix, in the early 1950s

Scottsdale was a small town with mostly dirt streets. The author's wife, Mary (nee White), is the daughter of Scottsdale's first Mayor, Malcolm White. During her father's administration Scottsdale was coined "The West's most western town." It has since grown to a world-renowned destination resort with about 250,000 residents. Baseball Hall of Fame pitcher Jim Palmer of the Baltimore Orioles graduated from Scottsdale High School in 1962. George H.W. Bush's Vice-President, Dan Quayle, was also a Scottsdale High graduate.

<u>Friday, March 2, 1951 (Second Round)</u>

Miami   104
Scottsdale 51

Miami won by 53 points. Two years later, in 1953 with a 23-1 record, Scottsdale won the State Class B Championship by beating Phoenix Carver 55-54.

The Republic's banner read: "Miami Sets All-Time Tourney Records By Crushing Scottsdale Quint, 104-51." The article read:

> It was the first time a state prep team, Class A or B, had scored 100 points in tourney play. It was possibly the first time the century mark has been reached in any game played in the University of Arizona's 'Bear Down' gym.
>
> Miami's sparkling performance overshadowed the rest of tourney play....
>
> Eli Lazovich led the unstoppable Miami attack by scoring 33 points and came near setting some records of his own. Lazovich has now scored 999 points in his playing career at Miami High. He needs only a single

point in the rest of the tourney to set a new school record, and possibly a statewide record for a high school player.

Miami ... now has a 100-point average for the [first] two games.

[Miami] set the record by leading 29-15 after the first eight minutes; 49-24 at halftime; 82-37 at the end of the third quarter. Coach Ernest Kivisto used subs most of the second period and frequently throughout the rest of the game.

The third game, against Clifton, was not so easy.

<u>Saturday, March 3, 1951 (Semi-Finals)</u>

Miami   72
Clifton   58

The Silver Belt described the game as "a credit to the Vandals, who proved they could play championship ball even when trailing by an uncomfortable margin." It added:

Right from the start, the Trojans stuck within two or three points of the Vandals, until early in the third quarter, when a spurt of baskets put them eight points in the lead. Coach Kivisto admitted, "They had us scared for a minute."

Coach Kivisto must have been more than "scared for a minute." The Tucson Daily Citizen (March 3, 1951) reported:

Just like Pima before them, Clifton was on its way to upset the Vandals. They, too, slowed it down and took the ball out of bounds instead of shooting the free throws. Clifton used a sliding zone and kept its guards back to stop the Vandal's fast break…. Miami led … at the half 32 to 20. In the locker room Coach Kivisto let the team have it. He yelled and cussed at them: "You are throwing away everything we worked so hard for!" He walked out of the locker room and did not go to the bench at the start of the third quarter. After Coach Kivisto left the locker room the boys started to yell and blame each other. Cuss words in Spanish were thrown back and forth. The boys regrouped and went out to start the third quarter but Coach Kivisto was not at the bench. He showed up minutes into the third. At the end of the third quarter Miami was ahead 48 to 43. It was still anyone's ball game. But Miami began to pour it on during the fourth quarter…."

The Vandals won by 14 points.

That set the stage for what many had awaited since the season's outset – a confrontation with Phoenix Carver High School. In a game that remained close, but which Miami mostly led throughout, the Vandals won, capping their perfect season with the State Class B Championship.

Saturday, March 3, 1951 (Finals)

Miami   58
Phoenix Carver   50

Lazovich scored just 7 points, and Acevedo 6. But Trujillo scored 19; and, with 13 from center Rudy Moreno, and, off the bench, 10 more from Leigh Larson, also a center, the Vandals held off the talented Monarchs.

A Phoenix sportswriter noted: "Carver's three-man zone defense (which beat Nogales) didn't work against Miami -- but the Vandals' mass guarding, which smothered other tourney rivals, didn't stymie Carver, either...."[38] He cited Carver's coach as saying Miami's reserve strength told the story.

The Silver Belt reported:

> Carver resorted to a trick long familiar to the Vandals -- taking the ball out of bounds instead of shooting free throws. This was partly responsible for their keeping Miami down well below its usual 90 or 100 points a game.
>
> The other reason for the low score was the effective bottling-up job which the Monarchs did on the Vandals' two top scoring aces, Eli Lazovich and Lupe Acevedo.
>
> .... Their lack of individual scoring honors, however, served to point up the fact that the Vandals are a wonderfully balanced team working as a unit and not as individual stars.
>
> Carver managed to keep nipping Miami's heels with a large number of extra-long field goals and some neat work under the basket tipping in rebounds.

As reported in the Republic, the AP release from Tucson read:

> Miami proved it had everything, including height, ability and fight, Saturday night in defeating a

---

[38] Bob Allison, *Along the Way*, The Phoenix Gazette, March 6, 1951.

determined Carver quintet, 58-50, before 2500 fans to win the Class B basketball title.

Forced to the limit, mighty Miami proved they were one of the best Class B prep teams in the state's history....

Credit was heaped on Ernest Kivisto, Miami coach, for producing a team that could click in the clutch when its two high scorers, Eli Lazovich and Lupe Acevedo, were bottled up....

[T]he Vandals [led] 26-25 at halftime. Lazovich had been kept to four points and Acevedo to a single basket in the first half.

In Class A, Mesa upset Phoenix Union 48-41.

State Tournament Recap
Miami 4 wins / 0 losses
Average Points Per Game:
Miami   82.5
Opponents   57.2
Average Victory Margin: 25.3

Season Recap

Miami   27 wins* / 0 losses
(* Officially, Miami had 29 wins, as Fort Thomas forfeited twice.)

Average Points Per Game:
Miami 84.7 (National Record) / Opponents 44.7

Average Victory Margin: 40

Lazovich Points: 562 (20.8 Per Game)
Acevedo Points: 497 (18.4 Per Game)
Trujillo Points: 469 (17.3 per Game)

Post-Season

Tucson sportswriter Ray McNally wrote that "the play in this class B meet was some of the finest I have seen" and that "the Miami-Carver finale was the best yet."[39] Putting aside his "natural Texas pride" he added, "the play here was superior to that of the Lone Star State. Particularly Miami and Carver."

Calling the Vandals "one of the greatest prep basketball teams in Arizona's history," the Tucson Daily Star stated: "Never before, and perhaps never again, has one high school team assembled together so much natural ability, spirit, and determination as the Vandals."[40] The article cited Miami's "superb physical condition" and observed that they were "a wonderfully balanced team working as a unit and not as individual stars." It added:

> [T]he Vandals were the snappiest dressers both on and off the court. In uniform, of course, the Miami lads are flashy in their white and green satin outfits. But even off the court, they were easily the best-dressed group at the tournament.

The article cited Coach Kivisto as saying he would "never have another bunch of boys like these. They were the 'dream team.'" It concluded:

> Sports editors and coaches were overwhelming in their praise for Kivisto's boys. Comments ranged from "The best team in Arizona's history" to "with a little more height they could give any college team in

---

[39] Ray McNally, *Sportingly Yours*, Tucson Daily Citizen, March 6, 1951.

[40] Arizona Daily Star, March 8, 1951.

the nation a rough battle."

The following Thursday, Miami's Silver Belt reported:

> One of the greatest prep basketball teams in Arizona's history brought a stunning climax to its unblemished season last weekend when Miami's Vandals swept through the State Class B Tournament in Tucson to emerge the state champions ....

The Silver Belt noted:

> While the other teams were wearing Levis, the Vandals were decked out in suits and ties. "They're real gentlemen," commented the manager of the hotel at which they stayed.

The almost universal praise was not shared by one Phoenix coach who had seen them play just once. The week after the State Tournament, the Republic's W. Jay Burk, in *"Rounding Up State Sports,"* wrote:

> Coach Runt Goddard took a quickie trip to Tucson last Saturday morning just to watch Miami's title-bound Vandals in action. The Phoenix Tech mentor was back in Tempe that night and was not overly impressed with the Kivisto Kids. "They use a sideline press with three men," the Hornet analyst said. "They are suckers for a mid-court pass. It seems to me they take advantage of inferior opposition, but a good team would stop 'em."

> "Goddard's wrong," Glen Barlow, assistant Arizona State College [now Arizona State University] basketball coach, said, "It is too bad he didn't stay

down to watch Miami in the finals. He would have seen them use entirely different tactics against Carver." Barlow was right -- Miami did change its style to suit the clever defense cooked up by Joe Flipper, Monarch mentor....

In beating Carver handily, Miami rose to the heights befitting its unbeaten march to the finals. Carver had a veteran array, one that had beaten Goddard's own Tech ball club, West Phoenix's up-and-coming Thunderbirds, and St. Mary's Knights (twice). The Birds and Knights had both beaten Mesa, two-year Class A titleholders. Carver had the shooters in Hadie Redd and Bertrand Russell to match Eli Lazovich (1,000 points) and Lupe Acevedo. Miami's high-powered scoring was checked, but Miami still won the game and title.

Miami has been the talk of Arizona for the year. Now let Miami be the toast of Arizona. It is time for fans, coaches, and players from all corners of this state to wave their 10-gallon hats and laud a really great team. The Kivisto Kids are high on the ladder -- we salute a fine team.

The following Sunday, Mr. Burk wrote:

Runt Goddard and Ernie Kivisto broke bread together Saturday during the coaches meeting here. We weren't so sure that the youthful Kivisto, Miami's great basketball mentor, would feel so kindly toward the affable Goddard, who has been around these scholastic diggings for many a moon now. However, the two were palsy-walsy, which makes our apology for Runt in this corner somewhat late.

> …. We quoted him Thursday and left out the fact that Runt said: 'Miami has a mighty fine ball club.' Now we said it, and that makes it official, for Goddard, nor this corner, had any intention of subtracting one iota from the Vandals remarkable record of the year….

Kivisto was named Class B Basketball Coach of the Year by the Arizona Coaches Association. Eli Lazovich and Lupe Acevedo were named to the ten-person Class B All-State first team. Six of the eight others (Hadie Redd and Bertrand Russell of Phoenix Carver; Lavon Norton of Pima; Bill Wanless of Nogales; Ed Karges of Holbrook; Frank Lujan of Clifton; and Charles Compton of Flagstaff) were on teams the Vandals beat.

After the season, the Silver Belt reported:

> Miami High School's nationally famous basketball team was forced to turn down an invitation this week to play in the American Legion National Basketball Tournament at Natchitoches, Louisiana.
>
> The ruling came from the Arizona Interscholastic Association, which prohibits all members from participating in post-season games.

The report stated that the Vandals were the third team invited to the 16-team event.

In the April 23, 1951, issue of Sparks News Magazine, former University of Michigan halfback and College Football Hall of Famer Tom Harmon penned an article titled *Champs of the Hardwood* in which he wrote:

> Because no national tournament is played in the high

school division, U.S. basketball fans were denied the pleasure of seeing in action what might well be the greatest prep-school basketball team ever assembled—the Vandals of Miami High School, Miami, Arizona.

The 1950-51 season record of Miami under young, affable Coach Ernie Kivisto: Games won, 27; Lost, 0. Season score: Miami 2,289 points; Opponents, 1,209 (including divisional and state tourneys). This sets a new national record (season's average per game: 84.7 for Miami, 44.7 for opponents). Against Morenci (Feb. 8, 1951) the Vandals set another state and national record for single game points (130). Guard Lupe Acevedo set a national record for points scored by a guard in a single game (56 against Duncan, Arizona – previous holder, Gerry Rald of East Chicago, Ind.) ....
The Miami record is by far the best wordless argument I have ever seen for a national prep school tournament in which champions for the east, south, north and west could meet at a place like Madison Square Gardens and play off for a national title....

.... [T]eams like this don't just happen. They are the reflection of a great coach who commands the respect and loyalty of his players.

Ernie ascribes Miami's sensational success to two things, strategy and training. He says, "We press our opponents to tire them out..." and adds: "I have very strict training rules...."[41]

---

[41] A copy of the Spark's article and photos that accompanied it is printed in *Pena* at 154.

Closing Perspective

To put the Vandals accomplishments in further perspective relative to the scoring climate of the times, in 1951 the Rochester Royals won the National Basketball Association championship by defeating the New York Knickerbockers 79 to 75 in the seventh game.

George Mikan, proclaimed the NBA's player of the first half century, set an NBA record by averaging more than 27.4 points a game. Alex Groza was second with an average of 23.4. The third highest average was 17.8; and the twenty-fifth was 11.6.

Dick Groat of Duke, who was the leading collegiate scorer, averaged 25.2 points a game.

For perspective in comparison to a 48-minute NBA game, playing just 32-minute games, with no shot clock, no dunking, no three-point shots, and opponents able to take the ball out of bounds rather than having to shoot free throws:

- Miami's 130-point game projects to 195,
- Its 122-point game projects to 183,
- Lupe Acevedo's 56-point game projects to 84,
- Eli Lazovich's 50-point game projects to 75, and
- Fito Trujillo's 45-point game projects to 67.

It seems unlikely that three different players from the same team will again break a state's single game scoring record during the same season, much less within one month.

It is fitting that Coach Kivisto have the last word about his once-in-a-lifetime team. Twenty-six years and more than 500 wins after he left Miami, and after his election to the Illinois Coaches' Hall of Fame and selection as IBCA Coach of the Year, he wrote:

> The 1951 Miami High School team was without a doubt the best high school team I have ever seen or coached, even today. They would fast break any team I have ever seen, coached or will ever coach. I shall always be thankful for that great opportunity to coach such a dedicated group of fine boys. My four years at Miami High School are memories I shall forever value and treasure. These were my four most rewarding years…. These boys played to win and gave 100 per cent in every way. It was the finest defensive team I have ever seen in the history of high school basketball. I have never seen that type of pressure man for man and fast breaking. I was very fortunate to be at Miami when I was blessed with the finest, dedicated talent any coach could ever ask for.[42]

---

[42] Arizona Silver Belt, January 6, 1977.

The Vandals' Legacy

As basketball moved from the 1940s into the 1950s, the game was evolving. It was still common to occasionally see two-handed set shots and under-handed free throws. Dunks were illegal and the jump shot was just coming into vogue. Free throws didn't have to be shot. It would be decades before there were three-point shots. Eli Lazovich's primary weapon was a one-hand set shot -- almost a platform shot from the top of his shoulder. The game was much slower than that we have come to know since.

For the most part, the athletes were smaller, too -- not as tall; not as big; not as strong; and they were slower and less agile. The half-court game predominated.

As a coach, Ernie Kivisto was at the vanguard of change; and his Vandals were among the first to successfully employ it. Their offense began at the opposing basket and continued at a fast pace to theirs. On defense, they badgered their opponents every step of the way. Their amazing success quickly led others to change their style of play and, within the next few years, scores that would have seemed fantasy (other than for Miami) in 1950-51 were becoming common.

Coach Kivisto and his Vandals were to high school basketball the equivalent of Roger Bannister's four-minute-mile. Thought to be undoable, once they did it, others soon followed.[43] But the Vandals were among the first.

---

[43] Thirty-two years later, Globe High School's 2003 Class 3A State Championship Team was 33-0, exceeding Miami's remarkable 27-0 season. But the Vandals were at the vanguard of run and gun basketball, and after their amazing season rules were changed to facilitate faster paced games and to make scoring easier.

EPILOGUE

The molten slag cooled. Its red-hot glow faded to pale orange and slowly disappeared. Bathed for a brief while in the ebbing afterglow, once again the western night sky was dark.

For thirteen brief, glorious weeks, something unique, something extraordinary, had happened in the copper and turquoise rich mountains of east-central Arizona. Almost unnoticed at first in the populous central valley to the west, week by week, game by game, brief reports filtered out -- often too late for the Phoenix papers.

With Phoenix sports reporters focused on the eagerly anticipated arrival of the New York Yankees for spring training -- with Joe DiMaggio, Yogi Berra, Casey Stengal, and promising rookies Mickey Mantle, Whitey Ford, Gil McDougald and Bill Skowron -- and on the shocking news of point-shaving by basketball powers City College of New York and Long Island University (with national scoring leader Sherman White among those charged), the sketchy reports of Miami's victories were at first under-reported and little noticed.

Belatedly, there occurred a dawning awareness that something special was happening in the mountains a hundred miles east of Phoenix -- that a small mining town of just a few thousand people had produced a basketball team that was scoring at a rate never seen -- a team that set a national scoring record; a team with three players who, within four weeks, successively broke the state's single game scoring record and who, individually on multiple occasions, had scored more points than entire teams were scoring in winning efforts elsewhere.

Having been slowly alerted by belated news of what already had occurred, and failing to fully comprehend its magnitude until the season neared its end, few outside the mining and farming communities of east-central Arizona and the Mexican border towns of Bisbee and Nogales, saw and had the opportunity to appreciate the magnificence of what may have been, at the time, the most exciting, efficient and effective basketball scoring machine ever -- a team on the cutting edge of high intensity, pressure-defense, little dribble, fast-break, run-and-gun basketball.

From Phoenix in the west and Tucson in the south, the red-hot glow beyond the mountains was at first too far away, and from a distance too faint, for Arizona's major population centers to realize and appreciate the scale of what was happening. Only at the end -- at the state tournament in Tucson -- were players, coaches and fans from throughout the state able -- for four games -- to view one of high school basketball's most amazing teams.

Appendix 1

More About Coach Kivisto and His Family

East Moline, Illinois

After Miami, Kivisto coached at United Township in East Moline, Illinois – one of the "quad-cities" on the Mississippi River across from Davenport, Iowa. Steve Tappa reported that "Kivisto coached at UT from 1951 to 1967, compiling a 232-154 mark and was inducted into the school's Hall of Fame in 1997." On that occasion, Bill Alee wrote in Davenport, Iowa's Rock Island Dispatch Argus:

> The more things change throughout the years, the more they also remain the same, according to Kivisto.
>
> "I've never had any problems coaching players. They've all been the same for me in that I get them to work hard and they learn discipline. I have the kids and the parents sign a contract so they know exactly where they stand and what's expected of them," said Kivisto.
>
> "The kids can't date during the week, only on weekends, and I try to get to every player's church, or take an individual to church if he doesn't have one. It doesn't matter to me what denomination they are."
>
> "I try to get all my kids to college -- 174 of my players have earned scholarships -- and my teams will always be competitive."
>
> If Kivisto speaks as if he's still coaching, it's because he is.

Oh, maybe not on the high school level anymore, but he's constantly on the go giving clinics and helping organize teams all over the world, such as when he coached a Finnish national team to a European title. He has also coached in Sweden, Czechoslovakia, Mexico and Canada.

Aurora, Illinois

He next coached at East Aurora, Illinois -- 42 miles west of Chicago -- from 1967 to 1982. In a February 2003 special to the Chicago Tribune, Patrick Z. McGavin wrote:

> At East Aurora his record is unassailable. In his 15 years there, his teams compiled a 309-94 record. In one four-year stretch, his teams qualified for the Elite Eight three times. His 1972 team finished third in the Class AA tournament; the 1969 Tomcats team was fourth.

While there, his teams were reportedly ranked in the Illinois Class AA Top Ten for 10 of 16 seasons; and he took his teams to the Illinois State Tournament three times. His 1979 team was reported by Bill Allee of the Rock Island Dispatch-Argus to have set an Illinois state record by averaging 93.5 points a game.

In July 1978, Coach Kivisto joined Arizona State University's Coach Frank Kush, for whom Sun Devil Stadium is named, in conducting the Ernie Kivisto Basketball Camp and the Frank Kush Football Camp for the Miami YMCA.

Later

At age 60, Coach Kivisto returned to Arizona in 1982 to become the basketball coach in Globe, Miami's arch-rival. Reportedly, he was then the third most winning active high school basketball coach in America.

He later coached in Texas where he is understood to have finished his career.[44]

In 2003, Sean Moeller of the Quad-City, Davenport, Iowa Times wrote:

> Former United Township basketball coach Ernie Kivisto was a salesman.
>
> He sold the game of basketball.
>
> Throughout his five decades as a coach and teacher, Kivisto extended his boundless enthusiasm for the game to kids who walked the halls of high schools he worked at in Illinois, Arizona and Texas.
> ....
> Throughout his coaching career, Kivisto opened up the game and had his teams play an up-tempo brand of basketball similar to the 1990's Running Rebels of UNLV, that still was new at the time. His 1979 Aurora East squad, while racking up a 25-3 record, scored over 100 points in 11 of its games — the second-highest total in Illinois state history.

---

[44] Bob Kivisto states that at Shawnee Mission, "Coach" was nominally the assistant coach, but functioned as the head coach. Bob tells of having called his dad after a hard-fought 119 to 114 loss to a heavily favored powerhouse from a much larger school. Knowing how disappointed Coach must have been to have come so close without winning, Bob asked his dad what he said to his players after the game. Coach said he told them: "I am so proud of you. If you would've scored just six more points we would have won." That exemplified, even in defeat, Coach Kivisto's positive, upbeat attitude and can-do coaching style.

> "Back then, when you mentioned Ernie Kivisto, everyone who knew Illinois high school basketball knew who he was. He was a whirlwind."....

Long after Coach Kivisto's retirement, Daily Herald columnist Jeff Long penned a 2010 article titled *"Some 28 years later he's still inspired by Kivisto's greatness."* He referred to Coach Kivisto as "the legendary, Hall of Fame basketball coach whose fun-and-gun style of play – and effusive personality – brought a uniqueness to high school sports not seen before or since." He noted that "more than a quarter of a century since he last coached, Kivisto remains a defining symbol for Aurora basketball." Referring to a former team manager (Paul Parks, "a successful rock-and-roll concert photographer in San Diego"), he stated:

> Kivisto used to pick up Parks in the early morning each day. Those rides often traversed the east side, with Kivisto pulling up to players' homes and knocking on doors to make sure they'd get to school and/or practice.

Describing Kivisto, he stated:

> [T]his was a guy who had "12+7+4" stitched on his red coaching shirts, the measure of devotion he expected toward basketball from his players – 12 months a year, 7 days a week, 4 hours a day. He advised his players to sleep with a basketball. And to keep them in good health, Ernie often provided oranges and loaves at practice.
>
> A whirlwind of exuberance, Ernie made crazy characters look boring in comparison.

Ernie was a Hoosier legend as well. Just recently, Parks had the opportunity in San Diego to speak backstage at an awards banquet with Bobby Knight. ... [T]he former Indiana coach raved about Kivisto's historical impact on prep basketball in Illinois...."

Bob and Tom Kivisto

First with Bob and then Tom, Coach Kivisto's 1968-69, 1969-70 and 1970-71 teams compiled an 81-15 record at East Aurora (26-7; 27-4; 28-4). His 1968-69 team ended its season in the Illinois State Championship semi-finals. Led by Tom, his 1970-71 East Aurora team averaged more than 110 points a game for the season's first ten games.

Both Bob and Tom were featured by Sports Illustrated in its "Faces in the Crowd," and both later played for the University of Kansas.

At Kansas, both Bob (in 1971) and Tom (in 1974) played in the NCAA Final Four.

Bob: A top-notch defensive specialist and the starting point guard at the University of Kansas on its 1971 Final Four team, Bob Kivisto's Basketball Museum of Illinois Biography reads:

Robert Kivisto holds the unusual distinction of being an All-State Player at two different high schools. From 1964-67, Bob attended (East Moline) United Township High School where he earned the honors as a junior. Bob set a national record with 52 points in a game as a freshman player. Kivisto played his senior year at East Aurora High

School where he had one of the best seasons a prep ever could. He scored 796 points, grabbed 298 rebounds, made 309 assists, and had 272 steals. For his four-year, 96 game career, he scored 2,052 points (21.4 ppg); grabbed 651 rebounds (6.8 rpg); distributed 743 assists (7.7 apg); swiped 645 steals (6.7 spg). After his prep career, Bob attended Kansas University, where he was on an NCAA Final Four team in 1971 with fellow IBCA Hall of Famer Dave Robisch (1973 inductee). After his playing days, Bob turned to coaching, spending time at several schools including being an assistant at Quincy University in Illinois and back at Kansas for a brief time.

As a coach, Bob Kivisto compiled a 227-80 record at Independence College in Kansas[45] and later coached at Aurora East. His 1999 East Aurora team was 20-9 and earned a spot in the Illinois State Tournament, losing to Schaumburg H.S. 60-54 in overtime.

Late that season, titled "ROAR AT EAST AURORA JUST LIKE OLD TIMES," Barry Temkin wrote for the Chicago Tribune (Feb. 12, 1999):

> Most kids don't appreciate having dad around all the

---

[45] The Indy Pirates athletics website states:

> In nine years of coaching, Bob Kivisto became the all-time winningest coach in the history of the Independence Community College men's basketball program—a mark that still stands to this day.
>
> From 1982-91, Kivisto recorded an incredible mark of 227-80, which included two 30-plus win seasons. His Pirate squads won seven Jayhawk Conference-Eastern Division championships. They also won the Region VI championship in both 1983 and 1984 to land a spot at the NJCAA National Tournament in Hutchinson. During his tenure at Independence, Kivisto coached five NJCAA All-Americans.

time, especially when they're doing what he used to do where he used to do it.

East Aurora head basketball coach Bob Kivisto swears he doesn't mind it. That's fortunate for his sanity because even though his father, Ernie, is retired and living in Texas, he's just about everywhere when it comes to Tomcat basketball.

....

"I can't keep track of everybody," Bob said, laughing. "I'm surrounded. I get stories all the time."

Ah, the stories.

Stories about Ernie, who talked 100 miles an hour and whose teams played the same way, piling up at least 100 points in a game 11 times in one season alone. Stories about the bottomless energy and enthusiasm that made him a legend just as much as did his 312-119 record and three Elite Eight berths in 15 years at East Aurora.

There was Ernie and his twin philosophies, the three D's (dedication, determination and desire) and 12+7+4 (practice 12 months a year, seven days a week, four hours a day).

And there was Ernie and his morning practices. Ernie calling parents to be sure his players were in bed by curfew. Ernie and his rules about haircuts.

"They always love to tell the stories, and I love to listen," Bob said. "I get fired up."

Bob was a senior in 1967-68, his dad's first season at

East Aurora.... So he was familiar with the school's rich basketball tradition and was eager to come home ....
While Bob brought back his dad's uptempo offense, he is not Ernie Jr. He shares his father's passion for the game and habit of stomping his foot in disgust, but he can't match Ernie when it comes to flamboyance.
....
Bob, though, is starting to match his father's success. East Aurora was 10-16 in Bob's debut but is 19-1 and ranked fourth in the Chicago area this season. A big reason for that prosperity is Bob's willingness to embrace his father's legacy rather than fight it....

As of 2019, no longer coaching, Bob was teaching English at East Aurora.

Tom: At last inquiry, Tom Kivisto still held the University of Kansas single game assist record (18) set in 1973. He was a member of KU's 1971 and 1974 NCAA Final Four teams. In 1974, he was drafted by the Carolina Cougars of the American Basketball Association. In 1977, he was inducted, as a player, into the Illinois Basketball Hall of Fame. His East Aurora HOF bio reads:

Tom Kivisto once scored 56 points for East Aurora High School against Rock Island. This was the highest of the four times he scored 50+ points. Tom was more than just a scorer. He set school marks that lasted for years in points, steals, forced jump balls and rebounds. Tom was an all-state player and an All-American Player as his team made two state finals appearances in 1969 and 1970. Tom went on to play for

Kansas University where he was team MVP twice and captain on the NCAA finalist team in 1974. Tom won the Big Eight Medal for the Best Scholar-Athlete and was named to the Academic All-America team ....

Until July of 2008, Tom was the President and Chief Executive Officer of SemGroup, L.P., a hugely successful oil and gas industry company headquartered in Tulsa, Oklahoma. At one time, Forbes magazine ranked it 14th among all privately held U.S. companies. Under his leadership, SemGroup reportedly completed more than 40 acquisitions and its total assets grew from $227.4 million in 2000 to more than $3.6 billion at year-end 2005. In 2008, almost overnight, SemGroup found itself in Chapter 11 bankruptcy after $3.2 billion in trading losses -- a victim of the sudden freakish rise in oil prices to more than $145 a barrel. Previously, in 2005, Tom had pledged $12 million to help fund KU's new practice football facility at Memorial Stadium. Reportedly, $4 million of that was funded before the SemGroup bankruptcy.

Accolades

Coach Kivisto and his sons Bob and Tom may be the only father-son triumvirate to have been individually featured by Sports Illustrated in its "Faces in the Crowd." SI wrote:

- "**Bob Kivisto**, the only freshman ever to play first-string basketball in the tough Mississippi Valley Conference, scored 52 points -- 70.4% of his shots -- for the East Moline (Ill.) High Panthers, to better by 10 the conference single- game scoring record." (March 8, 1965)

- "**Tom Kivisto**, 6'3" guard for East Aurora (Ill.) High, scored 51 points in a 98-80 victory over St. Charles High, breaking the Upstate Eight conference record of

45 set by his brother Bob in 1968. Against Fenton High, Tom hit 54, two better than Bob's school mark." (February 9, 1970)

- "**Ernie Kivisto**, 50, basketball coach at East Aurora (Ill.) High, won his 500th victory 86-80 over St. Charles. In 27 years as a head coach he has won 77% of his games and taught seven high school All-Americas. He has a 106-22 record in four years at East Aurora." (January 17, 1972)

In 1973, Coach Kivisto was a charter inductee into the Illinois Basketball Hall of Fame; and, in 1979, he was the IBCA High School Coach of the Year.

In 2001, Joe Henricksen of the Oswego, Illinois Ledger-Sentinel wrote: "Even before Tubbs, Tark and Marymount, my first introduction to up-tempo, fast break basketball was the legendary Ernie Kivisto and East Aurora."

When Coach Kivisto died in 2003 at age 81, sports columnist Bill Kindt of The Beacon News in Aurora wrote an award-winning column about the death of "Legendary East Coach Kivisto." According to The Beacon News, "when Ernie Kivisto coached basketball at East Aurora, Tomcats' games featured one of the hottest tickets in town."

Two weeks after Kivisto's 2003 death, Patrick McGavin wrote in a special to the Chicago Tribune:

> Al McGuire was rarely one to suffer by comparison, but when he crossed paths with Ernie Kivisto in 1981, his only option was to cede the floor and deflect the NBC cameras to the flamboyant, controversial high school basketball coach as part of his halftime show.

The ultimate basketball junkie, Kivisto revealed on the telecast his absolute devotion to coaching basketball "12-7-4" – 12 months a year, seven days a week, four hours a day.

Though Kivisto last coached an Illinois high school game more than 20 years ago, the frenetic style of play he favored and his outsized personality still evoke vivid memories. He was a veritable showman during an era in which high school basketball's popularity in Illinois soared.

....

At East Aurora from 1967 to 1982, Kivisto orchestrated a blistering, high-wire, full-pressure style of basketball that was infectious to watch – unless, of course, you were the opposing team he was bent on destroying....

....

Beginning with his own sons, Bob and Tom, Kivisto developed one prolific scorer after another.... During a 1980 game against DeKalb, Kevin Avery scored 51 points, and Robert Meeks added 44.

....

At East Aurora his record is unassailable. In his 15 years there, his teams compiled a 309-94 record. In one four-year stretch, his teams qualified for the Elite Eight three times. His 1972 team finished third in the Class AA tournament; the 1969 Tomcats team was fourth.

....

Coach Kivisto termed "success in coaching" as "turning your boys into fine young men, into good citizens, into Americans we can be proud of." A former player stated: "[A]s much as he loved basketball, he loved kids more. I loved playing for him. He'd do anything for you." He was "always coaching -- pushing buttons, trying to make people better."

In February 2019, East Aurora High School hosted the 9th Annual Ernie Kivisto Hoopfest in his honor.

Appendix 2

Miami's Players[46]

Lupe Acevedo:

5'10" 155 pounds / Senior / Starting guard

Boy's State 3
Football, 1,2,3,4; All-State 3; Co-Captain 4
Basketball 1, 2, 3, 4; All Conference 3, 4; All State, 3, 4
Abe Bernstein Award

---

[46] The information herein is based on multiple sources including Miami High School and the 1951 Concentrator (the Miami yearbook), the 1955 ASC-Flagstaff (NAU) La Cuesta (the Lumberjacks' yearbook), interviews with and information provided by "Fito" Trujillo, Andy Rumic and others, newspapers and media sources, obituaries, on-line research, and information obtained by "Sonny" Pena. *See* note 21, *supra*. His book refers to the Miami players at pages 17-19 and 185-186.

Pena states:

> His father, Antonio, was born in El Paso, Texas and his mother, Loreto, in Ascencion, Chihuahua, Mexico. They came to Miami in the late 1920s. His father worked in construction for different mining companies. His mother was a homemaker….

In game 15 against Duncan, Lupe set the Arizona single-game scoring record of 56 points, breaking the record set in game 10 by his team-mate, Eli Lazovich. He was first team All-State in both his junior and senior year.

He attended ASC-Flagstaff (NAU) on a basketball scholarship and is a basketball member of the Northern Arizona University's Hall of Fame.

In 1955, he joined Fito Trujillo and Nogales' Oscar Islas in leading the Lumberjacks to a 79-72 win over the University of Arizona Wildcats who were led by his former team-mate, Eli Lazovich, and Carver's Hadie Redd. He graduated in 1955 with a degree in education.

After graduation, he taught until retirement in the Pinetop-Lakeside-McNary area of the White Mountains of Arizona.

Lupe died in 1993, at age 60.

Scheduled again as of October 11, 2020, at Pinetop-Lakeside's White Mountain Country Club, the 35th Annual Lupe Acevedo Golf Tournament is held in his honor to benefit the Blue Ridge Scholarship Fund.

Elias Delgadillo (Huerta):

5'9" 150 pounds / Senior / Backup Guard

Senior Class President
Freshman Class Treasurer
Honor Club 2, 3
Football 1
Basketball 1, 2, 3, 4
Baseball 2, 3, 4

Elias was born in Morenci, Arizona.

In nearby Duncan, Arizona, his mother was a housekeeper for the parents of retired Supreme Court Justice Sandra Day O'Connor.

Later, in Miami, his father worked for Miami Copper Company and his mother was a homemaker.

During his high school years, he worked for a dry cleaner and delivered groceries for Miami Commercial, the company store.

He attended ASC-Flagstaff (NAU) for one year, served in the U.S. Army, and later graduated from ASC-Tempe (ASU).

He taught in California for 41 years until his retirement in 1999.

Hector Jacott:

6' 170 pounds / Senior / Starting guard

| Football 1, 2, 3, 4 |
| Basketball 1, 2, 3, 4; Second Team All-Conference 4 |
| Tennis 1, 2, 3, 4 |

Hector's family emigrated from Mexico to El Paso, Texas, and then to Miami. His mother was a homemaker; and his father worked underground for Miami Copper Company. His father died of silicosis when Hector was just six. The family was on welfare for a time; and Hector worked at a dairy and a drugstore.

He attended ASC-Flagstaff (NAU) on a basketball scholarship for one year before serving in the Korean War. He was later a foreman at Inspiration Consolidated Copper Company, owned Jacott Memorials and made cabinets.

He was also an Arizona Interscholastic Association official.

Hector died in 2000, at age 68.

Leigh Larson:

6' 4" 185 pounds / Junior / Backup Center

Junior Class President
Basketball; Second Team All-Conference
Concentrator (Annual) Sports Editor

Of Scandinavian descent, Leigh was born in Miami but lived part-time in Globe where, just a few houses away, he was a friend of the author.⁴⁷ His father was a regional union representative at the copper mines in eastern Arizona and western New Mexico.⁴⁸ His mother was a homemaker.

Leigh graduated from the University of Arizona Law School and served as Nogales City Attorney and Santa Cruz County Attorney. He was named Arizona's outstanding county attorney in 1971.

Leigh died in 1991.

---

[47] It was Leigh's nearby house into which the author was taken when, in early grade school, he snapped his tibia. Later, at the University of Arizona in Tucson, Leigh and the author played city league basketball together on a largely law school team with some Globe teammates. At practices and in games, Leigh often surprised unexpecting teammates with quick, short, precision passes like those the Vandals used so successfully during their state championship year.

[48] Titled "Orville Larson dead at 80; led union miners 'out of the dark ages,'" Tucson's Arizona Daily Star quoted the head of Tucson's program to assist displaced miners as saying:

> He was one of the most significant men in the State of Arizona. He was the John L. Lewis of the copper mines [referring to the president of the United Mine Workers of America from 1920 to 1960]. He led the labor unions and the miners out of the dark ages into the sunshine by battling the copper mines to bring dignity and parity to the miners in Arizona.

Eli ("Ted" / "Teddy") Lazovich:

6'2 ½" 185 pounds / Senior / Starting Forward

Sophomore Class President
Basketball 1, 2, 3, 4; All- Conference Co-Captain 3, 4; All-State 3, 4, Captain 4
Baseball, 1, 2, 3, 4
Tennis 3
Lettermen's Club President 4
Senior Play 4

Of Serbian descent on his father's side, Eli was born in Miami to parents who immigrated to the United States in 1912, the year Arizona became a state. His father was a lawyer and judge in Gila County, Arizona. His mother was a homemaker.

His brother, Dushan, was a sports reporter for the Arizona Republic in Phoenix and, later, in San Diego.

In game ten against Clifton, Eli set the Arizona single-game scoring record of 50 points, breaking the record set in game nine by his team-mate, Fito Trujillo. He was the first Arizona high school player to score more than 1,000 points and was first team All-State in both his junior and senior years.[49]

He lettered three years in basketball at the University of Arizona. In his final game, he scored a then record 38 points against arch-rival ASC-Tempe (ASU). He was also a member of the Wildcats' District Seven Champion and NCAA finals baseball team.

He coached the University of Arizona's freshman basketball team to an 11-8 season in 1955-56.

With a degree in education, he taught for several years at a Phoenix elementary school before working for the Arizona Compensation Fund, from which he retired in 1993.

He is a member of the Phoenix Bowling Hall of Fame and once bowled a three-game series of 807 (including a 300 game).

Eli died in 2003, at age 69.

---

[49] Following Eli's 1st team All-State selection his junior year, the author was walking past Globe High School one night with Paul White (later a Phoenix dentist) who noticed a person crouched beside a parked car. Paul yelled, "Someone's letting air out of tires. It's Eli Lazovich, All-State ….!" That's as far as Paul got. Eli jumped up and chased us up some nearby steps to the unlocked side-door of the high school, where we quickly disappeared into the darkness inside. Despite the commotion in his unlit, deserted hallways, "Blondie" Price, the school janitor, didn't catch us either.

Alfred ("Al") Lobato:

6'4" 180 pounds / Junior / Backup forward

Al was born in Miami to parents who emigrated from Mexico. His father worked for Miami Copper Company and his mother was a homemaker. He worked summers for Miami Commercial, the Miami Copper Company store.

He attended ASC-Flagstaff (NAU) on a football scholarship for one year before serving in the U.S. Army. He later worked 42 years for a company that manufactured aircraft parts, retiring as a senior engineer in 1997.

Rudy ("Pelon") Moreno:

6'3 ½" 185 pounds / Senior / Starting center

Football 4, First Team All-State Tackle
Basketball 2, 3, 4, Second Team All-Conference
Track 2, 3, 4

Rudy's father was born in Mexico. In Miami he worked mining claims and as a laborer. His mother was a homemaker, who was widowed when Rudy was eleven. She made and sold tamales and did ironing to provide money for the family. Rudy shined shoes, set pins at a bowling alley and worked part-time for Miami Commercial.

He was a champion high jumper in track and attended ASC-Flagstaff (NAU) on a basketball scholarship. He played there for two years before entering the U.S. Army.

He worked 38 years for the Pinto Valley Mining Company near Miami.

Andrew ("Andy") Rumic:

5'10" 170 pounds / Junior / Back-up guard

Of Croatian descent on both his father's and mother's side, Andy was a first-generation American who was the product of an arranged marriage. His father worked for Miami Copper Company and his mother left when he was young. After that, Andy and his sister were sent to a boarding school in Phoenix where they lived for a time.

Andy then returned to Miami to live with his father. They lived in a small house with no indoor bathroom or hot water. Year-around, Andy slept outdoors on the porch regardless of the summer heat, winter cold, and rain or snow. It was not until he could do so at school that he could shower regularly. And it was not until he was 18 that he had a home cooked meal. Instead, he ate at a restaurant owned by a friend of his father. His father had no car.

Andy attended the University of Arizona where he played fullback for the Wildcats. Graduating with a master's degree in education, he coached football at Tucson's Rincon High School before retiring in 1989. Married for more than 60 years to Globe's Frances Ryan (one of the author's classmates), he retired in Tucson.

Adolfo ("Fito") Trujillo:

5'11" 150 pounds / Senior / Starting guard

> Basketball 1, 2, 3, 4; Second Team All-State; First Team All-Conference

His parents were born in Mexico. His father worked at the mine and his mother was a homemaker. Fito worked at a grocery. The family didn't have a car. The nickname, "Fito," is the diminutive form of "Adolphito," a term of endearment among family members. Literally, it means "little Adolph."

In game nine against Safford, he set the Arizona single-game scoring record of 45 points.

He attended ASC-Flagstaff (NAU) on a basketball scholarship, graduating in 1955.

That year, he joined Lupe Acevedo in leading the Lumberjacks to a 79-72 win over the University of Arizona Wildcats led by his former teammate Eli Lazovich and Carver's Hadie Redd.

He was the Lumberjacks' Most Valuable Player in both his junior and senior years and was the Frontier Conference's Most Valuable Player his senior year. That year, he was also a National Association of Intercollegiate Athletics All-American.

He is a basketball member of NAU's Hall of Fame.

At ASC-Flagstaff, he majored in accounting with a minor in Spanish, was vice-president of "Chain Gang" and was Secretary/Treasurer of the letterman's club.

Against Ohio's Rio Grande College at the NAIA Tournament, he recalls having held "Bevo" Francis, the nation's leading scorer who twice scored over 100 points in a game and who averaged a national record 48.3 points per game, to 27 points in a game the Lumberjacks lost.

In a U.S. Army Far Eastern Tournament in Japan, Fito held former three-time All-American Ralph Beard, who helped lead Kentucky to two straight NCAA championships, to just eight points in the first half and 24 for the game.

After his military discharge, Fito worked for and later purchased Globe Builders' supply. He also served as a member of the Gila County Board of Supervisors for several years.

Retired, Fito lives in Mesa, Arizona.[50]

---

[50] Fito's son, John Trujillo, was Gila County's Public Works Director for 10 years. Then, during a 15-year career with the City of Phoenix, he was the Assistant Public Works Director before becoming its Public Works Director.

Dick ("Dickie") Vargas:

5'10" 155 pounds / Sophomore / Backup guard

His father was a truck driver for Miami Copper Company and his mother was a homemaker.

He attended ASC-Flagstaff (NAU) on a football scholarship, graduating in 1957.

He returned to Miami as head basketball coach for 29 years. Before an estimated crowd of 9,000, his 1970-71 team (20-7) won the Class 4A state championship; and his 1980 (21-3), 1981 (16-6) and 1983 (22-0) teams won Class 3A state championships.

Jesus Romero, Manager:

His parents were born in Mexico and emigrated to Morenci before settling in Miami. His father worked for Miami Copper Company and his mother was a homemaker. They lived in a three-room shack with a dirt floor and had no means of transportation. He shined shoes and, summers, worked as a firefighter and in a lumber yard.

He taught, coached and was an administrator at a Phoenix elementary school until his retirement in 1989.

His 2011, age 80, obituary states:

> He was born in, Miami, AZ, raised in Turkey Shoot Canyon, attended Bullion Plaza and graduated Miami High School. He received his bachelor's degree in education from Arizona State University. He enjoyed a lifelong career as an educator and vice principal in the Isaac School district [Glendale, AZ] until he retired after 32 years of service. He took pride in being a Korean Veteran and his induction into the National

Hispanic Sports Hall of Fame for his athletic accomplishment as a member of the 1951 Miami Vandals Championship Basketball team.

Nick Ragus

Nick Ragus was Miami's athletic overseer during its record season. Illustrative of the schizophrenic relationship between Globe and Miami, he was born in Globe; and, conversely, John Pavlich, the author's junior and senior football and basketball coach in Globe, was born in Miami. Yet, each was intense regarding the Globe-Miami sports rivalry (see example in About the Author).

In 1947 and 1948, Ragus was the head football coach, and from 1947 through 1949 the head basketball coach, at ASC-Flagstaff (NAU). Before that, at Miami High School, Ragus had coached Pavlich. Ragus said of Coach Pavlich when he died:

> He was a dedicated coach, teacher and liked all youths and liked to work with them. He worked with them, lived with them, played with them and cried with them.
>
> Being the kind of man he was brought him three state football championships and three state basketball championships, a feat no other man in the state has accomplished. He also served his country in the best military manner that a man can serve.

That typified the respect those in Miami and Globe had for one another, despite their intensely partisan sports rivalries.

In a 2008 Globe Miami Times article regarding the many successful Globe-Miami "Viches" Bill Norman stated, "John Pavlich led Globe High School football and basketball teams to sequential years of victory. Nick Ragus was Miami High's answer to Pavlich."

He died in 1981. In lasting tribute, Miami High School is located on Ragus Road and the football field is Ragus Field.

Cheerleaders:

B. Escobedo

C. Warner

B. Aneas

Twirlers:

P. Lacy — M. Sendejas — O. Paddock — A. Reveles — M. L. Burleson

G. James — D. Torres — R. Roe

B. Starkey — R. Pacheco — C. Fletcher — E. Reveles — M. Evans

VANDAL TWIRLERS

Dating at Last

JUNIOR - SENIOR PROM

Appendix 3

Miami Practice Drills

The following drills were sketched by the author during a 1951 Miami practice at the Eastern Conference Tournament held in Globe High School's new gymnasium.

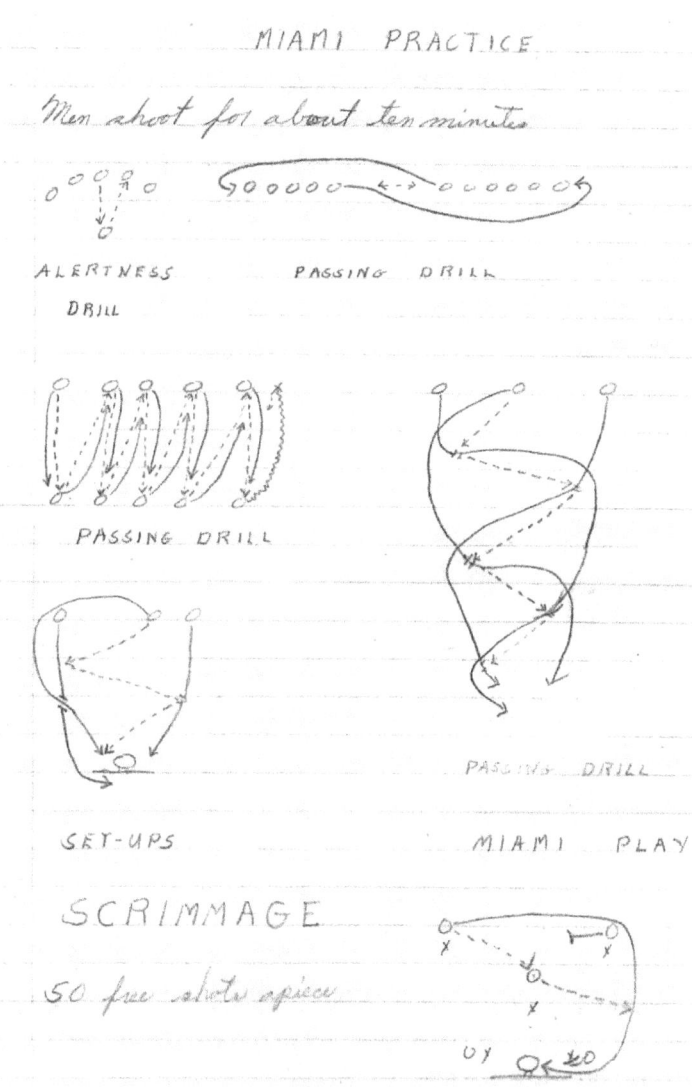

Appendix 4

Coach Kivisto's Post-Season Handout to Players

Coach Kivisto prepared and distributed to his players the following summary of the 1950-51 Miami Vandals' achievements (handwritten notes added by Fito Trujillo):[51]

COMPLETE RECORD OF THE 1950-1951 MIAMI HIGH BASKETBALL TEAM

EASTERN CONFERENCE-EASTERN DISTRICT-AND STATE CHAMPIONS

Compiled by Coach Ernest Kivisto

Unbeaten in 27 games

MIAMI HIGH SCHOOL SEASON AND TOURNAMENT RECORDS 1950-1951

DATE	NAME OF OPPONENT	OUR SCORE	OPPONENT'S SCORE
Dec. 9, 1950	St. Johns	78	41
15	Superior	63	41
16	Thatcher	87	39
21	Bisbee	74	35
22	Nogales	56	50
28	Flagstaff	101	28
29	Winslow	79	32
Jan. 5, 1951	Duncan	94	38
6	Safford	94	50
12	Clifton	122	56
13	Pima	56	26
19	Pima	80	21
25	Morenci	77	44
26	Clifton	92	72
27	Duncan	99	47
Feb. 2	Thatcher	57	39
3	Safford	72	43
9	Morenci	130	43
16	Globe	105	61
17	Globe	102	49
		1719	859

WON 20 LOST 0   AVERAGE PER GAME 85.9   42.9

---

[51] A copy of the handout was also obtained from Andy Rumic. Although Andy's copy was easier to read, the author chose Fito's because of the personal notes he added.

EASTERN DIVISION TOURNAMENT

Feb. 22, 1951	Safford	88	30
23	Globe	95	49
24	Pima	57	42
		240	121

WON 23 LOST 0   AVERAGE PER GAME   80   40

ARIZONA STATE TOURNAMENT

Mar. 1, 1951	Holbrook (First Round)	96	70
2	Scottsdale (Second Round)	104	51
3	Clifton (Semi-Finals)	72	58
3	Carver of Phoenix (Finals)	58	50
		330	229

WON 27 LOST 0   AVERAGE PER GAME   82.5   57.2

NEW NAT'L RECORD   SEASON'S TOTAL   2289   1209
                   SEASON'S AVERAGE PER GAME   84.7   44.7

The 130 points scored against Morenci, Feb. 9, 1951, is a new national and state record.
The 88 points scored against Safford in the Eastern district tournament was a new tournament record which broke the previous record of 83 against Ft. Thomas set in 1948.
The 95 points scored the following night against Globe broke the record again.
The 96 against Holbrook in the State meet was a new record for state play but was broken the following evening in the quarter-finals with 104 against Scottsdale. This is also a new record for the U. of A. gymnasium. This was the first team in the nation ever to score over 100 points in state tournament play.

MIAMI HIGH SCHOOL BASKETBALL ROSTER

NAME	AGE	YR.	YRS. EX.	POSITION	HT.	WT.
1. Lupe Acevedo	18	Sen.	4	G	5'10"	155
2. Elias Delgadillo	18	Sen.	2	G	5' 9"	150
3. Hector Jacott	18	Sen.	2	G	6'	170
4. Leigh Larson	17	Jun.	2	C	6' 4"	190
5. Eli Lazovich	17	Sen.	3	F	6'2½"	185
6. Alfred Lobato	18	Jun.	2	F	6' 4"	180
7. Rudolph Moreno	17	Sen.	2	C	6'3½"	185
8. Andrew Rumic	17	Jun.	1	G	5'10"	170
9. Fito Trujillo	18	Sen.	2	F	5'11"	150
10. Dick Vargas	16	Soph.	1	G	5'10"	155

INDIVIDUALS SCORING RECORDS OF FIRST TEAM

Eli Lazovich in 27 games has scored 562 points for an average of 20.8 points per game. This is a new Miami record and also a new state record. He held the former r of 421 set last year. This total was for 26 games. In the Eastern tournament he scored 30 points against Safford, 33 against Globe and 14 against Pima for a total of 74 points. A new tournament record. His 33 against Globe was a new individual record breaking the former of Mike Laughrin of Globe set in 1949. He also scored 50 points against Clifton for a new record which was later broken by Lupe Acevedo. He scored 88 points in 4 games at the state tournament for an average of 22 per game which was a new individual total for state tournament play. For the past two years he was selected to the First Team of the All-State Team. This year he was selected Tri-Capt. by his team-mates. Also, was named Capt. of the All-State Team. Scored 1027 points for an all-time state prep scoring varsity record. Chosen first team 2 yrs. on Conference and District team.

Lupe Acevedo holds the state record of 56 points in one game scored against Duncan. This is a national record for a guard. In 27 games he has scored 497 points which is a new record for a guard in the state, and also, a four year total of 849 points a new record for a guard in the state. His season's total gives him an average of 18.4 which is also a new state record, for a guard. For the past two years he has been chosen to the First Team of the All-State team besides first team for two season's on the Eastern Conference and District teams. He is the only 4 year letterman. Set a new state tournament record for a guard by scoring 34 points against Holbrook. Set individual record for a guard in state by scoring 69 points in 4 games. Elected Tri-Capt. by team-mates for season.

Fito Trujillo scored 45 points against Safford. He has a season record of 17.3 with 469 points in 27 games. He was selected to the first team of the Eastern Tournament team and to the Second Team of the All-State team. Lazovich, Acevedo, and Trujillo is the greatest trio of Arizona basketball having scored 1538 points between them. Elected Tri-Capt. for the season by his team-mates. Was voted the teams most improved player.

Rudolph Moreno scored 233 points for an average of 8.7 in 27 games. He was selected to the second team of the Eastern Tournament team. One of the best on rebounds. 2nd letter on Varsity.

Hector Jacott scored 156 points for an average of 6.5 points per game. Ace defensive man. Holding top opponent scorers to an average of 4.5 points per game. Was pace setter for Miami's fast break. Was selected on the second team of the Eastern Tournament team.

INDIVIDUALS SCORING RECORDS OF SECOND TEAM

Elias Delgadillo the only senior on the second team scored 98 points. Second year on the varsity. A guard and also senior class president.

Leith Larson a 6'4" junior was one of the most improved players on the team. He scored 147 points to rank 6th in scoring. Although a reserve he showed such playing ability that he was selected on the second team of the Eastern All-Tournament team. He also scored 40 points in the state tournament to set a new record for a reserve breaking the former record of 29. Also, missed by two votes in being selected on the second team of the state tournament selection. One of the most outstanding rebounder on squad.

Alfred Lobato another 6'4" junior who scored 66 points this season.

Dickie Vargas a 5'10" is the only sophmore on the squad. Scored 28 points.

Andy Rumic a 5'10" junior scored 27 points.

Fito's notes appear to read:

- Regarding himself: "Attended NAU" / "Graduated in 1955 w Degree in Education" / "All Conference Two yrs" / "Most Valuable Player (1954, 1955)" "Played 4 yrs of Varsity Basketball at NAU" / "Same as Lupe"

- Regarding Moreno: "Attended NAU one year. Enlisted in the Service 2 yrs"

- Regarding Jacott: "Attended NAU one year / Enlisted in the Service 2 yrs"

- Regarding Delgadillo: "Attended NAU one year. Enlisted in the Service 2 yrs" / "Came back and graduated from NAU w/Degree in Education"

- Regarding Lobato: "Attended NAU one year. Enlisted in the Service 2 yrs" / "Worked in [???] where he still lives / [???] Retired."

NATIONAL RECORDS HELD BY MIAMI HIGH SCHOOL
SET BY 1950-1951 TEAM

1. Set new national record for points scored in a single game by bucketing 130 points against Morenci on Feb. 9.
2. Average of 84.7 in 27 games to break former agerage of 70.1 also set by Miami in 1948.
3. Scored 970 points in 10 home games for an average of 97 per game.
4. Lupe Acevedo scored 56 points for a guard to break former record of 48.
5. First high school team to score over 100 points in state tournament play. Miami 104 over Scottsdale 51.
6. In state tournament play scored 330 points for an average of 82.5.
7. First high school team to score over 100 points in 6 games and also scored over 90 in 6 games.
8. Had three time outs to opponents 125 in 27 games.
9. In 27 games outscored the opponents by an average of 40 points per game.

STATE RECORDS HELD BY MIAMI HIGH SCHOOL
SET BY 1950-1951 TEAM

1. The above as well as being national records are also state records.
2. Eli Lazovich scored 562 points for a new one year total for the state.
3. Eli Lazovich scored 1027 points for a new three year total.
4. Lupe Acevedo scored 497 points for a new one year record for a guard.
5. Lupe Acevedo scored 849 points in a four year total for a new state record for a guard.
6. Lupe Acevedo holds individual state scoring record of 56 points in one game.
7. Lazovich, Acevedo, Trujillo have scored 1538 between them.
8. Broke individual scoring record three times in one season. Trujillo--45, Lazovich--50, and Acevedo--56.
9. Scored 1267 points in conference play for an average of 90.5 in 14 games.
10. Have taken 12 timeouts in four year period to opponents' 474.
11. Only team in state to win 4 consecutive undisputed conference championships and 4 district championships.
12. Longest home win streak in the state of 51 games still unbroken.
13. Longest conference win streak in the state of 61 straight still unbroken.

STATE RECORDS CONTINUED

15. First undefeated season in the history of Miami High School and Eastern Conference.

16. Coach Ernest Kivist's record of 95 wins against 8 losses in 4 years best prep record in the state.

17. First time in the history of the state that the same two players have made the First Team of the All-State Team two years in Succession. Eli Lazovich and Lupe Acevedo.

18. Scored 2289 points in one season for new state record.

THE CODE OF A SPORTMAN

Keep faith with your team-mates-Always
Keep your temper-Always
Keep yourself fit-Always
Keep a sound soul and a clean mind and a healthy body-Always
Keep your pride under in victory-Always
Keep a stout heart in defeat-Always
Play the game-Always

Appendix 5

Miami Players at Arizona State College - Flagstaff

Several Miami players, including Lupe Acevedo, Elias Delgadillo (Huerta), Al Lobato (on a football schoarship), Rudy Moreno, Fito Trujillo and Dickie Vargas (on a football scholarship) attended Arizona State College in Flagstaff (now Northern Arizona University). Because of the Korean War some left for military service. The Lumberjack's 1955 yearbook pictured Trujillo and Acevedo.

Lupe Acevedo

"Fito" Trujillo – Miami
Who's Who in American
Universities and Colleges
Associated Men Student's
Counsel, President
Chain Gang, President
A-Club, Secretary-Treasurer

Lumberjack Basketball

The yearbook stated: "This year's Lumberjacks will probably go down into the school's annals as one of its greatest teams. The team finished with a regular season record of 19-3. In conference play they had an 11-1 record."

The references below to "ASC Tempe" and "Tempe" are to what is now Arizona State University at Tempe.

Big Art Henriksen, 6-10, towers over Fito Trujillo (4), 5-10, and Lupe Acevedo (3), 5-10. Fito led the team in scoring field goals, and also set the individual scoring record with 35 points in the ASC Tempe game. Lupe led the team in having the fewest fouls called against him and free throw percentage. He was high scorer last season. Art led the team in offense rebounds.

THE FOUR SENIORS ON THE TEAM

Fito Trujillo, John Gladis, Buddy Islas, Lupe Acevedo

Fito, Keagle award winner as Arizona's athlete of the month in January, and most valuable player in the conference tournament, averaged 15 points a game, made 49% of his field goal attempts, 68% of his free throws, and got 161 rebounds. He scored 35 points against Tempe.

John averaged 6.3 points per game, made 40% of his field goals, 54% of his free throws, and got 11 rebounds. In the Lumberjack 111-79 victory over Highlands, John made 17 points in the second half.

Buddy averaged 8.8 points per game, made 44% of his field goals,

65% of his free throws, and came up with 78 rebounds. Buddy's greatest number of points this year was 20 in the game with Adams State.

Lupe averaged 11.5 points per game, made 39% of his field goals, 69% of his free throws, and got 59 rebounds. Lupe led the team in scoring in six games and had the honor of never fouling out of a game.

Lumberjack Track and Field

Left to Right: Lalo Serrano, Bill Hannah, Fito Trujillo

Appendix 6

Dr. Marin's Social Commentary

Published in *The International Journal of the History of Sport*, Dr. Christine Marin has written an insightful essay titled *Courting Success and Realizing the American Dream: Arizona's Mighty Miami High School Championship Basketball Team, 1951.*[52]

---

[52] A native of Globe, Christine Marin, Ph.D., is Archivist/Historian at ASU's Dept. of Archives and Special Collections in the Hayden Library. She has described herself as:

> a lucky kid growing up on Euclid Avenue on the west side of Globe in the 1950s. The street was a dirt street, no sidewalks. Euclid became an *arroyo* after a hard and fast rain. It was a United-Nations-kind-of-street. Italian, Mexican American, African American, and a sprinkling of Serbian families lived on Euclid Avenue, a true multi-cultural and working class neighborhood.

With her permission, the author has quoted extensively from her essay, omitting footnotes.

More recently, *The Journal of the Emeritus College at ASU* has published *Courting Success and Realizing the American Dream by Dr. Marin*. It is well worth reading in its entirety. It can be found on-line at Emeritus College Journal - ASU, or at:

> https://emerituscollege.asu.edu/sites/default/files/ecdw/EVoice10/courting_success.html

In track at Globe, the author's teammates included Dr. Marin's two brothers, Ben and Tom Marin. Tom was a conference champion high jumper; and Benny was a distance runner who while in 8th grade ran a 5:07

Dr. Marin examined "how third-generation Mexican-Americans and their hard-driving high-school basketball coach in Miami, Arizona, promoted Americanization, achieved success and won the 1951 state basketball championship."[53] She noted:

> They attended a segregated elementary school and experienced integration at the high school. As teammates with Euro-Americans and victors on the basketball court, they established cordial friendships and facilitated better ethnic relations in their school and in their copper-mining-based community. Many attended college and escaped a working-class environment and achieved upward mobility....[54]

She added:

> On its way to the state championship, Arizona's only unbeaten team, from the copper-mining town of Miami, shattered national high-school single-game scoring records in 1951. Through their play, competitive spirit and success, they gained the

---

mile. At state his freshman year he finished 2nd in the mile run with a time of 4:46.5. As a sophomore, he won State with a 4:46.4 mile. That year, he ran a 4:35.2 mile at the Arizona Relays, finishing in a dead heat for 1st. As a junior, at State he won the mile in 4:34.9 and the half mile in 2:01.9. His senior year, he lowered his mile run time to *4:32.2* at the Arizona Relays while finishing 2nd by a tenth of a second. Benny later competed in track at ASC-Tempe (ASU); and he coached track and field at Globe High for 39 years. A member of the Arizona Hispanic Sports Hall of Fame and the Globe High Hall of Fame, he coached 31 individual state track champions and in 1987 was named the Arizona Track and Cross-Country Coaches Association Coach of the Year.

[53] Vol. 26, No. 7, June 2009, 924-946, at 925.

[54] *Ibid.*

admiration of their community and improved ethnic relations in the copper town that set them apart because of their ethnicity.[55]

For perspective, she noted:

> Basketball was important to Miami. Mexican-American boys were introduced to the game at young ages, usually by YMCA youth leagues that pitted Mexican-American teams from the Mexican Y against the YMCA's Euro-American teams....[56]

Bullion Plaza was the segregated elementary and junior high school that Miami's Mexican Americans were required to attend. Dr. Marin quoted a former Miami player (Tony Gutierrez):

> We were tough kids that grew up tough. At Bullion Plaza, the older guys put up a fight just to see what would happen. Times were tough too. Everyone was poor. Besides, *Mexicanos* had to be tough to be able to put up with what the *gringos* did to them.[57]

Regarding his transition to Miami's integrated high school, she noted:

> [H]e soon discovered that his love of basketball helped him overcome any negative experiences. Basketball made him feel like a winner among his white peers. And he liked that: "We were better than

---

[55] *Id.* at 926.

[56] *Id.* at 928.

[57] *Id.* at 929. The on-line Merriam Webster Dictionary defines *"gringo"* as a "foreigner in Spain or Latin America especially when of English or American origin; *broadly*: a non-Hispanic person."

them as athletes and that's when they started to like us. They wanted to win. And they needed us *Mexicanos* to win," he said.[58]

Regarding Ernie Kivisto, Dr. Marin said:

> Kivisto tested the agility and the determination of his new team and the boys endured his grueling practices daily. They learned his fast-break style of play ...: fast break on offense and the full-court press on defense. Elias Delgadillo explained the method:
>
>> One of the keys to the fast break is the pass. The object here is to get the ball down court as quickly as possible. To accomplish this, the passes had to be quick, crisp and accurate. [Kivisto's fast break style] was quite different from the standard style of the time of setting up for a shot in play.

She added:

> Kivisto taught his team the floor routines he learned at Marquette. He reinforced the fundamentals of

---

[58] *Ibid*. The author's experience was different. From his perspective, probably because of the more difficult circumstances under which they grew up, the Mexican Americans matured earlier and tended to be tougher and better athletes in junior high school and the first two years of high school. But those advantages equalized as the non-Mexican Americans matured. For reasons different than those of the Mexican Americans, basketball and other sports also served as a confidence builder for the author whose then shyness and excessive self-consciousness was significantly dispelled by the experience of competing effectively with and being accepted by his Mexican American counterparts whose toughness and athletic prowess he respected and admired.

> basketball, with passing and pivoting exercises and shooting drills in their practices. Players took shots at the hoops from every angle and distance on the court. For conditioning exercises, he made the boys run laps around the gym and run sprints up and down the court. "We would run forwards, then sideways and then backwards with our arms extended in a guarding position," Elias Delgadillo emphasized. Kivisto taught them the importance of teamwork in competitive sports and that sports belonged to everyone....[59]

Coach Kivisto came to Miami in 1947. Tony Gutierrez was quoted as saying:

> Before Coach Kivisto came along, we wore those ivy-league shirts that players long before us were wearing. They were loose, all worn out and used again and again. But Kivisto fought for his team and insisted on new uniforms, new outfits, new shoes for his boys. The uniforms were white, like satin, silky-like, with long white or green warm-up pants. Our white jackets had a long square collar in the back that lay flat across the back of our shoulders. We were the first high school basketball team in the state to play in white tennis shoes, high tops. Every team at that time wore black low cut tennis shoes. We dazzled them. For some Mexican boys, it was the first time we had brand new shoes that we could call our own, and not some hand-me-downs from the *gringos*.[60]

Regarding Kivisto's first season in 1947-48, Dr. Marin noted:

---

[59] *Id.* at 930.

[60] *Id.* at 931.

> The Vandals averaged '61.5 points per game scored in 14 games. Kivisto claimed this average as a national inter-scholastic record, and Arch Ward, sports editor for the Chicago Tribune, backed that claim and cited the average of 49 points per game held by the Champaign, Illinois, high school team as the existing record in 1947....[61]

After winning the Eastern Conference championship, the Vandals lost in the semi-finals at state.

Noting Kivisto's "distaste for racism," Dr. Marin cited Tony Gutierrez's description of an incident at Morenci in January 1948:

> [W]e went to a restaurant that wouldn't let us in. There was a sign on the window that said, 'No Mexicans Allowed.' Kivisto got mad.... We didn't eat there. He said that we were a team and that if we couldn't eat together, then no one would eat.
> ....
> [H]e became a hero in our eyes. There were other *gringos* who felt the same way that he did. We wanted to win games for him. So did the *gringos* on the team. That experience brought the school and maybe the town together because soon everybody knew what the coach had done....[62]

In 1948-49, the Vandals again won the Eastern Conference championship but lost in the semi-finals at state.

Regarding Coach Kivisto's third season, Dr. Marin noted:

---

[61] *Id.* at 931-32.

[62] *Id.* at 932-33.

> At the end of the 1949-50 seasons, the Vandals' record was 24 wins and only two losses, while averaging 84.7 points per game. In March 1950, they won their third successive Eastern Conference championship....[63]

But again, Miami lost at state to "a stronger adversary in the Nogales Apaches."[64]

Regarding Kivisto's final season, Dr. Marin noted:

> Kivisto entered his last season as head coach of the Vandals in 1950-51. Led by the seniors Lupe Acevedo, Rudy Moreno, Hector Mario Jacott, Alfred Lobato, Elias Delgadillo and Adolph 'Fito' Trujillo, ...predominantly a Mexican-American team, became the All-American sports heroes whose victories remain embedded in Miami's sports history even 58 years later.[65]

---

[63] *Id.* at 934.

[64] *Ibid.*

[65] *Id.* at 934. Other teammates were:
- "Dickie" Vargas, who later coached the Vandals basketball team to multiple championships,
- Eli Lazovich, of Serbian descent, who led the team in scoring, who in week six set the Arizona scholastic scoring record with 50 points (broken two weeks later by Acevedo with 56), and who (with Acevedo) was 1st team All-State for the second straight year,
- Leigh Larson, of Scandinavian descent who, off the bench, scored 10 critical points in the state championship game, and
- Andy Rumic, of Croatian descent.

> The portraits that emerge of [those Mexican American players] bear similarities. Their families immigrated to Miami from New Mexico, Texas, Sonora (Mexico) and Morenci, Arizona, in the mid-1920s and early 1930s. Their fathers labored in the local copper mines. The youths came from working-class and impoverished backgrounds, they attended the segregated Bullion Plaza Elementary School; and all were reared under difficult economic circumstances. Single parents reared three of them: Lupe Acevedo, Rudy Moreno and Adolph 'Fito' Trujillo. Loretta Apodaca Acevedo died in 1944 from tuberculosis when Lupe was 12 years of age. Francisco Moreno and Refugio Trujillo died of silicosis in 1944 and in 1948 when their sons, Rudy and 'Fito', had reached the ages of 12 and 16.... When the Miami Trust Company plotted the West Live Oak Addition in 1947 and redeveloped its properties for the sake of tourist dollars, the company evicted and relocated the Acevedo and Moreno families to the company's properties elsewhere in Miami.[66]

Dr. Marin notes that Miami's high scores were not without controversy.

> High scores against opponents characterized Miami's relentless drive for [the state championship]. They scored over 100 points against five competitors in their 1950-51 seasons. The high scores delighted Miami fans. Opposing teams, however, criticized Kivisto and his squad for showing little mercy on its weaker opponents.
>
> When the Vandals' 122-58 score against Clifton

---

[66] *Id.* at 935.

proved humiliating for the Trojans and their fans, [their coach] chided Kivisto for purposely running up Miami's score in order to satisfy his own ego, to establish his school's records and in order to enhance his reputation. The controversy over Miami's high scores became weekly fodder for Arizona's sports writers from Phoenix, Clifton, Globe and Miami, who debated the matter in the press. The writer for the Copper Era, representing the eastern regions of Clifton, Morenci and Duncan suggested that all 'Eastern Conference schools should boycott Miami and forfeit each game' in order to throw a wrench in Miami's scoring average. The ire of Clifton's sports fans reached a fever pitch when Coach Kivisto received anonymous letters containing death threats against Miami's scoring aces Lupe Acevedo and 'Fito' Trujillo. The letters warned him to 'expect physical violence during and after the [next Clifton] game'....

[The] editor of Globe's Arizona Record, took a matter-of-fact position in his defense of Coach Kivisto and his players for their competitiveness and athleticism for playing hard and clean basketball – the kind that attracted attention from College basketball recruiters and coaches:

> Most members of the rampaging Vandal squad come from families definitely not in the upper income brackets. It's hardly a secret that colleges offer basketball scholarships to outstanding material. And if a scintillating prep record can mean a college education to a few kids who otherwise might not have been

so fortunate, what's wrong with that?[67]

Regarding the Mexican American ethnicity of Miami's team and its African American state finals opponent, Dr. Marin noted that the minority players on both teams had attended segregated schools, "the Bullion Plaza Elementary School and Carver High School," and had competed against each other for a state basketball championship.[68]

She also noted that "a newspaper in Helsinki, Finland praised the accomplishments of Ernest Kivisto, 'a coach of Finnish extraction',"[69] that former Heisman Trophy winner Tom Harmon had stated that he did not "know of any high school in history ... that could seriously challenge Miami's performance," that a Tucson sportswriter had called the Vandals "the best team in Arizona's history," and that, "speaking at a post-season banquet in Miami, the coach of Loyola University in Los Angeles had offered scholarships to five of the Mexican-American Vandals."[70]

---

[67] *Id*. at 936-37. Those comments were prescient. Five of the Vandals' Mexican American players received scholarships to and played basketball at ASC-Flagstaff (NAU). Eli Lazovich received a University of Arizona scholarship. Each of the Vandals is understood to have attended college.

[68] *Id*. at 937.

[69] *Ibid*.

[70] *Id*. at 937-938.

Appendix 7

Miami's Opponents

George Washington Carver High School:

Carver was Phoenix's all-Black segregated school. That was before the United States Supreme Court ruled in its landmark 1954 *Brown vs. Board of Education* decision that "in the field of public education the doctrine of 'separate but equal'" was "inherently unequal" and ordered desegregation "with all deliberate speed." Before that, in 1953 the Arizona Supreme Court had ruled that Arizona's 1909 segregation law was unconstitutional; and earlier in 1954 it ruled that segregation in elementary schools violated the 14th amendment. The United States Supreme Court cited those Arizona cases in its landmark decision. Perennially, Carver was an athletic powerhouse. Following its loss to Miami in the 1951 state championship game, Carver won the state championship in 1952, was runner-up in 1953, and won again in 1954. During those four seasons Carver won 93 games while losing just 18.

The March 19, 2021 Arizona Republic featured an article by Dana Scott titled *Paving the Way* (subtitled *Segregation built Phoenix Carver High, but sports helped remove boundaries, create integration*). Noting the difficult environment for blacks, it stated:

> In that environment, the Carver Monarchs basketball team thrived.
>
> In 1951, it made the championship game in its state class, losing 58-50 to undefeated Miami, which had a large Hispanic student body. In 1952, the first under Leon Jordan, it made it back to the title game and won, defeating Ajo 65-49. The Monarchs returned in '53, losing to Scottsdale High in a tight game, 54-53.
>
> It's final championship came in 1954, when Carver downed Duncan, 47-39.
>
> Then everything changed.

Hadie Redd (Phoenix Carver):

The mainstay of Carver's state championship runner-up team, Hadie Redd joined Eli Lazovich as a member of the University of Arizona Wildcats' basketball team. When Lazovich set the Wildcats' scoring record of 38 points, Redd added 20.

The University of Arizona's athletic web page states: "From 1953-55, forward Hadie Redd was a top scorer for the team, becoming a two-time All-Border Conference selection, and the first African American letter winner for the U of A."

In 1992 he was inducted into the University of Arizona Sports Hall of Fame. His plaque reads:

> The University of Arizona's first black letterman in both basketball and baseball, leading the way for others to come. Led team in scoring both seasons at Arizona and received All Border Conference honors each year. Following military service, entered law enforcement in San Francisco, soon being named to San Francisco Police Department's First Police Community Relations Unit. Moved to the San Francisco District Attorney's office in 1956 and quickly earned the reputation as an outstanding investigator. In 1971 was appointed Chief Investigator, the first black person to hold such a post in the state of California. Still held that position at time of induction.

With Lazovich, he was also a member of the Wildcats District Seven champion and NCAA finals baseball team.

Charles Christopher (Phoenix Carver):

Termed by Republic columnist Dean Smith "one of the greatest athletes ever developed in Arizona high school ranks," Charles Christopher was elevated as a freshman to Carver's 1950-51 varsity basketball team. He is pictured after his selection as Captain of the 1953 Class B All-Tournament team. As a senior he led the Monarchs to a 24-1 season.

He died at age 20. While attending ASC-Tempe (ASU), he was the Sun Devil basketball team's leading scorer when after an injury his heart stopped during routine surgery to repair a broken wrist. Before that, as a freshman he had played in 12 varsity games and was averaging 12.9 points a game.

ASU established the Charles Christopher Trophy, awarded to a freshmen athlete with outstanding athletic ability, scholarship and personal qualities.

Porfirio "Buddy Islas" (Nogales):

Buddy Islas joined several Miami players at ASC – Flagstaff (NAU). He, Lupe Acevedo and Fito Trujillo graduated in 1955 after having helped lead the Lumberjack basketball team to a 19-3 season. His senior class photo bio reads:

> Buddy Islas – Nogales
> Associated Men Student's Counsel
> Chain Gang

He later became an educator and Principal, teaching in Nogales and Pima Community College for 45 years.

Morenci High School:

Morenci High School

In 1976, the Morenci Wildcats scored 132 points against Sahuarita south of Tucson, thus exceeding the 130 points Miami scored against Morenci in 1951.

Morenci's football field was cut into the side of a mountain, with one end zone near a drop off. When teams scored at that end of the field, they went to the other end to kick extra points. Otherwise, the ball would go down the hillside. Globe's Coach Pavlich told of a game at Morenci in which he played for Miami while in high school. The fans had harassed the Vandals when their bus arrived and had continued doing so during the game. Late in the game the Vandals were ahead and closing in on another score near the goal line at the hillside end. Instead of running a play they quickly punted the ball out of the ballpark and down the hill.

In 1966 the "Morenci Nine" joined the Marines to fight in Vietnam. Only three of those young men returned. Their story generated national publicity and is recounted by Kyle Longley in *The Morenci Marines*, available on-line. Referring to Morenci as "a place where cultures intermingled," the description states that "the nine friends included three Mexican Americans and one Native American."[71]

---

[71] Similarly, in 1967 the author's half-brother, Greg Gibbons, was one of 19 NAU Sigma Nu fraternity brothers who enlisted in the Marines. In Vietnam, Greg was at the Khe Sanh hilltop base during the 77-day siege by a People's Army of Vietnam force of approximately 20,000. Greg was awarded the 1st of three Purple Hearts when hit by shrapnel there when the ammo dump blew. His 3rd Purple Heart was awarded after he stepped on a land mine a few months later while preceding his squad across a rice paddy dike shortly before his 21st birthday. After hospitalization on Guam, Greg returned to Phoenix where with the Police Department he was successively assigned to motorcycles and the SWAT Team and sometimes worked undercover narcotics until his retirement. On a Swat Team assignment, he was shot while aiming his pistol, but the bullet that would have hit him in the face instead hit the weapon frame and deflected to his hand.

Appendix 8

Globe High Profiles

Max Spilsbury:

With his Holiday Bowl NAU Players

Max Spilsbury, one of those to whom this book is dedicated, was the most inspirational man I ever met. Tall and slender, with an athletic physique, an engaging smile and personality, and handsome despite a nose broken many times, he was also one of the toughest men I ever met.

Raised since infancy in Mexico, Max moved to Bisbee, Arizona during junior high school, just across the border from Naco, Mexico. As a junior, he was Arizona's Class 3A football Player of the Year in 1942.[72]

He enlisted in the Marines and became a Marine Raider.[73] A family member related that Max was with the 4th Marine Raider Battalion and that on the island of Guam in the Marianas was shot in the knee on July 28th, 1944.

Even among his fellow Marine Raiders, Max was memorable. Recounting Max's and his unit's activities on Guam, another Marine states:

> Ever since we hit the area we had been taking covetous glances at a tempting piece of Jap booty that lay ahead of our lines. It was a Jap gun of approximately 40 mm caliber and would help bolster our night lines. Finally Private first Class Max R. Spilsbury, Colonia Juarez, Mexico, spoke up, pointing at the gun. "How about it Goheen," he said. Lieutenant Goheen had told us that if we called him

---

[72] Max related that, while sitting on the bench during his first year of football at Bisbee, some impatient fans began chanting "We want Spilsbury! We want Spilsbury!" Hearing the chants, venerable coach Waldo Dicus called out: "Spilsbury!" Max grabbed his helmet and putting it on, ran to Coach Dicus who turned, pointed to the stands, and said, "Spilsbury! Get up there!"

[73] There were multiple groups of Marine Raiders under different commands. The 1943 movie "Gung Ho" (the Raiders' motto) memorialized the raid by Carlson's Raiders on Makin Island. The term has been described as meaning "work together" or, aptly as respects Max, "unthinkingly enthusiastic and eager, especially about taking part in fighting or warfare."

Lieutenant or sir in the battle zone he would turn around and salute us. "The Japs," he said, "like nothing better than to shoot an officer, and I don't intend to be shot."

Lieutenant Goheen told Spilsbury, "Go ahead. Get a couple of BAR [Browning Automatic Rifle] men and four or five rifle men to cover you though."

Four of us went forward to get the piece. Spilsbury threw a couple of grenades at the Japs laying around the guns to make sure they were dead and we walked into the position....

Two of us picked up the gun, the other two the ammunition. Walking back was hard. We expected every moment to get a bullet in the back.

But we returned safely and set up the gun in the mounting darkness. The Japs did not attack that night, but the blackness was hideous with hand grenades – our own. A man to our right was sure the Japs were sneaking up on him so from dusk to dawn we crouched low in our foxholes listening to bits of metal whiz above.

Morning finally came. Max looked rather quizzically at the Jap gun. "You know," he said, "I guess I should be happy that the Japs didn't hit us last night, but I'll be dammed if I wouldn't be happy to have used that gun against them." [74]

The account then recalled harrowing details that followed.

---

[74] Found on the internet at *usmcraiders.com*, the account is credited to Allen L. "Doc" Savage.

As a coach, Max was all about effort and will to win. Instead of favoring his stars, he heaped praise and love on those who exhibited those qualities. Some said that his enthusiasm, joy, and the *esprit de corps* he inspired at the high school level could never work at the college level, but it did. It worked at every level, even when, after having been wounded in combat, he himself was in college at the University of Arizona. During football games he often met his players coming off the field by running out to bear hug and swing them around – even players the size of John Mellekas a large UofA tackle who later played for the Bears, 49ers, and Eagles.

At the University of Arizona, with a metal plate in his knee, Max lettered four years in football and was team captain in 1949. He also played a year of basketball (1946-47), was heavyweight boxing champion, and was the all-around rodeo champion. Playing end in football, he was 2nd team All Border Conference in 1946; and was later named by a Tucson sportswriter to the UofA's mythical all-time team.

Max had quickly become a legend at the UofA; and his legend became embellished. In *Don't Bunch Up: One Marine's Story*, William Van Zanten, a rural Arizona Marine who later played for Max at NAU, wrote:

> Max had grown up on a working cattle ranch in northern Mexico…. Football and Max were made for each other…. He loved to hit and be hit. He was strong, fast and totally fearless….[75]

Noting Max's enlistment out of high school in the Marines and that

---

[75] Random House Publishing Group, at 72. Originally found on-line (with the quotations cited to that), this 4.3/5-star book is currently available on-line from Amazon and others.

he had immediately volunteered as a Marine Raider, "the toughest of the tough," Van Zanten recounted that Max had been shot in "both" knees [note 73, at 72-73]. He wrote:

> ... Playing football again an impossible dream? Not for Max. Somehow he found the courage to walk out onto the football practice field at the University of Arizona. College football provided yet another outlet for his love of contact and combat. He played end, on both offense and defense, even though he couldn't run the 40 in 10 seconds and his pass catching skills were almost as dreadful.... His mission during each game was to destroy any person with the wrong-colored uniform. He went about his mission with a sense of purpose that amazed and inspired his teammates and coaches.... [at 73-74][76]

Harry Varner and John Hobbs watch the play intently during the Salad Bowl fracas; Max Spilsbury concentrates on a comment from Governor Dan Garvey.

---

[76] Pictured with Max, John Hobbs was later Managing Parter at Jennings Strouss.

Several of Van Zanten's comments regarding Max's coaching style resonate with the author from his experience as one of Max's Globe Tigers:

- "Max felt that to play football well, you had to be able to endure pain, and to endure pain, you had to practice having pain. No amount of physical contact in practice was sufficient to achieve perfection at hitting and being hit." [at 74]

    [We experienced that at Globe. Practices were tough. Games were a picnic. Playing for Max was a joy.]

- "[S]urviving Max's training camps and endless practice sessions drew us together in a very special way." [at 76]

- "Twice a day he took ... half the candidates and formed a single line starting 10 yards to his left. The other half formed a line starting 10 yards to his right. .... Every few seconds he blew the whistle. At the sound of the whistle the first person in each line charged forward into a violent collision with his counterpart from the other line. .... This procedure often resulted in match-ups with small wide-receivers facing much larger defensive tackle types, but it made no difference to Max. He wanted to see who did and who did not want to be hit, and keep on hitting. .... It was an excellent test for a love of contact and a willingness to bleed. Football skills could be evaluated later. He wanted to test a person's character first...." [at 101-102]

    [From the collision that resulted during such a drill,

when as a sophomore the then 150- pound author "form-tackled" a powerful 200+ pound senior tackle by driving my shoulder into his mid-section and pulling his powerful knees into my chest, I still have displaced cartilage. Things like that got Max's attention.]

- "At the end of every practice session, Max liked to get our attention with a string of 100-yard wind sprints." [at 104]

[Ours started at 50 yards and became progressively shorter. The author always tried to finish among the first and, although often dehydrated from August late-morning and early-evening "two-a-days" the author tried not to join those who headed for the water cooler afterward. I wanted Max to notice that.]

After graduating from the University of Arizona, Max came to Globe, where he coached football and junior varsity basketball in 1950 and 1951. He then returned to Bisbee where he had played his high school football. His 1954 Bisbee team won the Arizona Class B championship and four of his players were 1st team All-State. The year before, Globe's 1953 team that he initially molded before leaving for Bisbee had tied for the state championship. In effect, for two straight years teams he coached at different schools won the state championship.

After his stints at Globe and Bisbee, Max spent the 1955 football season as an assistant coach at the University of Arizona. At season's end, Abe Chanin titled his sports column in Tucson's Arizona Daily Star, "Arizona Losing Brilliant Homestate Coach…." He wrote:

It is rather remarkable that this 31-year-old student of football is being considered for the head coaching position at such schools as Brigham Young of the Skyline Conference and Arizona State at Flagstaff. After all, Max has had only one season of collegiate coaching and that, only as an assistant.

What does Spilsbury have that makes him so popular…?

…. Even bullets didn't stop him. Max had caught a Jap machine gun bullet in his knee and wore a silver plate. But he loved football and he wasn't going to let a war wound stop him.

…. His Arizona linemen this past season swore by him….

…. [W]wherever he goes, you can be sure he'll be carving a fine career. And there will be a lot of us, unhappy over his leaving, who will be cheering for his return.

Max accepted the head coaching position at Arizona State College at ASC-Flagstaff (NAU). In his first year, 1956, he took a team that was winless the year before to an 8-2 record, followed by an 8-1 season in 1957. During the 1957 season, Abe Chanin wrote:

Max Spilsbury has his own formula for making a small college football team go. It's his own variety of 'atomic fire' and he fills every one of his players with it until they explode against their opponents with fanatic fury….

Spilsbury doesn't have a great football team. The

team is made up mainly of Arizona high school players that neither Arizona nor Tempe [ASU] wanted....[77]

When a player comes off the field, Spilsbury runs over to him, rubs his hair, pats him on the back, shakes his hand and encourages him. The player, as phlegmatic as he might be off the field, becomes a burning, driving player.

In 1958, Max took a 10-0 team to the National Association of Intercollegiate Athletic Association's first national playoff, defeating Minnesota's Gustavus Adolphus 41 to 12 with what Abe Chanin termed "flaming desire, more than football ability."[78] Citing his "great 1958 football team," Governor Earnest McFarland declared December 6, 1958 Max Spilsbury Day in Arizona.

At St. Petersburg, Florida, in the nationally televised Holiday Bowl,

---

[77] That was not true of Globe's Cruz Salas. A member of ASC-Flagstaff (NAU)'s Sports Hall of Fame, Cruz described being "kidnapped" by Max from ASC- Tempe (ASU) where he was to be the starting fullback. Max told Cruz his mother wanted him to take care of his younger brother, Carlos, in Flagstaff. Carlos later started for the 11-1 1958 Holiday Bowl team. Cruz's NAU Hall of Fame citation reads:

> He led the Lumberjacks to a pair of Conference titles, and a combined 16-4 record over two seasons. In 1956, he led the squad in rushing with a then school-record 830 yards, and in 1957 led in rushes as the team played its first ever game at Lumberjack Stadium. He was named to the Frontier First Team All-Conference squad, and was a unanimous selection to the all-conference team for a second consecutive season.

[78] Van Zanten states that Max took "a failing football program at Arizona State College at Flagstaff, Arizona, ... to small college prominence in three years" and "kept it there on the strength of his will and personality." *Id*. at 71-72.

the Lumberjacks lost to Northeastern Oklahoma State 19 to 13 on a mud-slowed field during a rainstorm.

During the season, Tucson sportswriter Lou Pavlovich wrote:

> How does Spilsbury inject such tremendous spirit into his proteges?
>
> The answer seemed simple Saturday, after watching the former University of Arizona grid star guide his club on the sidelines. His every move was predicated on genuine friendliness and concern for his boys.
>
> Before the kickoff, he shook hands with every player starting the game. He stopped long enough to chat for a few seconds with each player.
>
> Several hours before the game, his entire football squad had attended a funeral for the father of one of their team members….
>
> Veteran football official Ralph Deal, one of the most respected officials in the southwest, said: "Max is a great spirit man…. He instills two important things into his players -- spirit and attitude…."
>
> What about his Lumberjack football players? What do they think?
>
> … [S]ays back Paul Renner, "I worship Max just like everybody else on this team…."[79]

---

[79] The author is among the many who in a sense worshipped Max. But for all the many good ways in which he influenced my life, there was one I regret. After the Globe Jr. Varsity played its last game against Miami a week

In 1983 Max and his 1958 team were inducted into the NAU Sports Hall of Fame.

Max Spilsbury (Football Coach, 1956-64)
The winningest football coach in Lumberjack history, his teams compiled a nine-year record of 59-24-5. Spilsbury's 1958 team compiled an 11-1 record, losing the NAIA Championship game to Northeastern Oklahoma State, 19-13. More than 40 of his players were All-Frontier Conference, and 15 signed professional contracts. He was elected to the Arizona Sports Hall of Fame in 1971. [80]

---

before, the varsity played in the 1952 conference tournament at Duncan. Wearing my new football letterman's sweater, I joined those who travelled to the game on a school bus. During the game, a tall, slender, attractive, blonde classmate and I became better acquainted. Although we ran in different circles and had not interacted socially before then, I had noticed her for some time. By the time we were ready to return to Globe -- about a 2 ½ hour trip on a narrow winding road -- she was wearing my week-old letterman's sweater and had invited me to sit with her in the back of the bus during the slow trip home. The door closed, the lights went out and the bus started. Then, suddenly, the lights came back on and the door opened. Max climbed onto the bus and, looking left and right, strode down the aisle until he found me with her in the very back seat. He said he had room in his station wagon and "invited" me to ride back to Globe with him. During the long ride back, he repeatedly commented impishly that my new letterman's sweater, which the gal I left was still wearing, would have "bumps in it." She ran with a cowboy crowd and I never again had the opportunity to be with her. To this day, I wonder what I missed and to miss what I think I missed. Whenever I hear the strains of the Four Seasons singing "Oh, What a night!" I am haunted by my unmet fantasy: "I didn't even know her name, But I was never gonna be the same, What a lady, what a night! .... [I]t ended much too soon...." Thanks, Max!

[80] Max remained NAU's winningest coach until, in his 17th season, Jerome Souers picked up his 60th win in 2008.

1958 Lumberjacks Football Team

Playing under the name of Arizona State College at Flagstaff, Max Spilsbury's 1958 squad made history when it became the first Arizona collegiate team to appear on a nationally televised sporting event - the 1958 Holiday Bowl from St. Petersburg, Florida. Although it lost that NAIA Championship game to Northeastern Oklahoma State, 19-13, the team finished with an 11-1 record, and a No. 2 national ranking.

In 2008, Max Spilsbury Field was established at Lumberjack Stadium.

While at NAU, Max authored *"Slot T Football"* (Prentice-Hall, Inc. 1961). Lynn "Pappy" Waldorf, then San Francisco Forty-Niners Director of Personnel, wrote the Preface. He termed Max "a man who brings imagination, good organization, and a challenging leadership to his approach to the game of football." He cited his players' "unusual pride in achievement," concluding that "anything … Max Spilsbury has to say on the subject of football, technical and otherwise, is well worth the close attention of his fellow coaches, players, fans and all who enjoy our greatest collegiate game." In the closing chapter, Max cited the intrinsic values of football, stating that participants learn that "through cooperation, hard work, and loyalty, victories will outnumber defeats." Terming football "democracy at its best," he added: "All men are equal on the field; each performs and is rewarded according to his abilities."

Published posthumously, Max also authored *"50 Years of Football"* which was edited by his daughter-in-law Debra Spilsbury.

In 1965, Max returned with his family to Colonia Juarez, Mexico. There, in part with used equipment scrounged from coaches in Arizona, he established a football program and brought teams north of the border to play small schools in eastern and southern Arizona. He coached football at the high school through the fall of 2000.

Max died in 2001 at age 77.[81]

---

[81] Max's son, Klinton, played the leading role in 1981's "Legend of the Lone Ranger."

John Pavlich:

John Pavlich, the other to whom this chronicle is dedicated, was born and raised in Miami, Arizona. Both parents were Croatian (Pavlic), having separately emigrated through Ellis Island from near Dubrovnik. Like the Kivisto family, his family has epitomized the American Dream of those who have adopted our culture and valued our freedoms.

After playing football for and graduating from ASC-Flagstaff (NAU), as a member of the Arizona National Guard (the celebrated "Bushmasters"), he fought the Japanese in the jungles of New Britain and Dutch New Guinea. General McArthur said of the Bushmasters: "No greater fighting combat team has ever deployed for battle."[82] On leave in Australia, Coach Pavlich met his future wife, Merle, who entered the U.S. as a war bride, debarking in San Francisco.

Coaching Globe's Tigers for 20 years – he won three state basketball championships (1960 22-5; 1964 22-3; 1967 26-2) and three state football championships (1953 9-1; 1956 9-0-1; 1957 9-1).[83]

---

[82] In January 1961, when assembled the morning after the author's arrival for the Infantry Officer's Orientation Course (*i.e.*, officer basic training) at Fort Benning, Georgia, a crusty, much-decorated Sergeant loudly called out whether anyone was from Arizona. The Sergeant proudly announced that he had been a member of Arizona's Bushmasters during WWII.

[83] Initially coached by Max Spilsbury two years earlier, the author played center on Coach Pavlich's 1953 football team that was the Arizona

Coach Pavlich is understood to be the only person to have coached both football and basketball at the annual Arizona All-Star Games; and he is a member of the Arizona High School Athletic Coaches Hall of Fame. He is also a member of the NAU Sports Hall of Fame and the Globe High School Hall of Fame. Coach Pavlich's Northern Arizona University Hall of Fame plaque reads:

> **John Pavlich (Football/Track, 1936-38)**
> Pavlich was an offensive and defensive tackle for the Lumberjacks. The 1938 Lumberjacks team was the only Arizona school to win a Border conference football game, defeating rival ASU-Tempe 19-13. Also participated in two field events, the discus and shot put. Coach Pavlich assisted Frank Brickey with the 1947-ASC varsity football squad. As both a high school basketball and football coach, his basketball record was 156-99 and his football record was 75 wins, 41 losses and 3 ties. He coached in McNary, Globe and Sunnyside (Tucson). He won the Football State Championship in 1953, 1954, 1957 and 1960 [instead, he won three, in 1953, 1956 and 1957]. His basketball teams were State Champions in 1960, 1964 and 1967. He was voted Conference Coach of the year in 1953, 1956, 1957, 1960, 1964 and 1967. He coached the Arizona High School All Star Football

---

Republic's Class B state co-champion. The other two were Phoenix Carver and Casa Grande, the only team to which Globe lost (by a point) and that later also lost a game (by a touchdown). Coach Pavlich's humor showed in a "compliment" he once gave me. My basketball assets were hustle, desire, diving for loose balls, passing and, with long arms and a wide wingspan, rebounding and defense – not shooting. In the game that sent us to State our junior year, I was fouled after a late game rebound and managed to make the go-ahead free-throw. In our locker room afterward, Coach Pavlich told the team, "I knew we would win when Keltner went to the line. He'd wish it in."

Game in 1954 and the All Star Basketball Game in 1960. Serving the youth of Arizona for 21 years, Pavlich is a member of the Arizona High School Coaches Hall of Fame.

Coach Pavlich left Globe to coach football at Sunnyside High School in Tucson, and he also became athletic director. He died in 1972, at age 54.

The Pavlich family has been remarkable and, like Miami Coach Kivisto's family, exemplifies how quickly and successfully immigrant families can assimilate and succeed.

Coach Pavlich's older sister, **Katherine (Pavlich) Duncan**, was Salutatorian of her Miami High School class and was later Valedictorian of her class at ASC-Flagstaff (NAU). There, she was also twice elected Homecoming Queen. Yet, when she first entered grade school she was unable to read and write English.

She and her husband (Clarence Duncan, a distinguished lawyer with whom the author was privileged to be a friend and partner at Jennings Strouss for almost two decades, and who during WWII flew the treacherous "Hump" over the Himalayas between India/Burma and China) were married for 67 years until his death.

The Goldwater Institute's Clarence J. and Katherine P. Duncan Chair for Constitutional Studies commemorates their devotion to constitutional processes and government.

Coach Pavlich's other sister, **Mary (Pavlich) Roby**, was the first Director of Athletics for Women at the University of Arizona. She later became the University's first female Associate Director of Athletics (for both men and women). The University of Arizona's "Mary Roby Gymnastics Training Center" is named in her honor. She is a member of the University of Arizona Sports Hall of Fame and the

National Association of Collegiate Directors of Athletics Hall of Fame. Her University of Arizona Hall of Fame bio reads:

> Was a letter winner during undergraduate years at Arizona, 1944-1948. Began her career as an athletic administrator at the UA in 1959 as Director of Women's Recreation Association. Was named the UA's first Director of Athletics for women in 1972 and became Associate Athletic Director for men's and women's sports programs in 1982. Held rank of full professor in Department of Exercise and Sport Sciences. Led UA Women's Athletics into the Intermountain, WCAA, Pac-West, and Pac-10 Conferences. Was a member of the Pacific-10 Conference Council from 1986 through her retirement, vice president of the Pac-10 Council in 1987-88, and a member of the Compliance Committee from 1987-89. Was a founder of the council of Collegiate Women Athletic Administrators and a member from 1979-89. Was vice president of AIAW from 1976-78 and chair of the AIAW Committee on Men's Athletics from 1977-1980. Served on the NCAA Professional Sports Liaison committee from 1981-87, and chaired the NCAA women's Committee on Committees in 1984-85. First woman selected to serve on the NACDA and US Sports Academy executive boards. Is a member of the Golden Key and the UA Mortar Board Hall of Fame.

John and Merle's children (**John**, a retired US Army CWO-5, **Gary**, a former teacher and coach, and **Paul**, a teacher and family business owner) have made their own contributions.

John and his wife Linda's two boys have both been teachers. **Jim** is Executive Director of Operations for the Montrose, Colorado School

District. **Mike** is Director of English Arts and English Learners for Sonoran Schools in Tucson. Both served in the Army -- Mike in Iraq as a helicopter pilot (CW2) and Jimmy (Cpt) in Bosnia and Iraq where he earned a bronze star.

Paul and his wife Peggy's daughter is **Katie Pavlich**, a University of Arizona graduate who by age 26 was news editor of Townhall.com. Katie has authored two books, *Fast and Furious: Barack Obama's Bloodiest Scandal and Its Shameless Cover-Up* and *Assault & Flattery: The Truth About the Left and Their War on Women*. She appears often as a host, co-host and panelist on Fox Cable News, including its popular weekday discussion shows *The Five* and *Outnumbered*. Their son, **Paul Ivo** is a bio-medical engineer.

Ken Troutt:

A University of Arizona graduate, Coach Troutt was a skilled student of basketball. Innately good-humored and funny, he coached for 30 years, first at Globe High School and then at Central High School in Phoenix, where his Bobcats won four divisional titles and he was named Divisional Coach of the Year twice. His 1957 Globe Tigers (25-2) won the Arizona Class A state championship. For Boys Basketball, he is a member of the Arizona High School Athletic Coaches Hall of Fame. He is also a member of the Globe High School Hall of Fame. He died in 2005 at age 79.

Coach Troutt's son, **"Kenny" Troutt, Jr.**, coached Glendale Cactus High School to an Arizona Class 4A basketball championship in 1994 and his teams were runner-up twice. Coach Trout's Arizona High School Athletic Coaches Hall of Fame bio reads in part: "Coach

Troutt's son, Kenneth, was inducted into the AHSACHOF in 2017 marking the first father/son duo to be honored in the same sport."

Ed Nymeyer:

Edwin ("Pudge") Nymeyer, who wrote the Introduction, graduated from Globe High School in 1954. As a GHS junior, he was selected to the five-man 1953 Class B state All-Tournament basketball team. He scored 44 points in one out-of-town game.[84] As a GHS senior, playing end on Globe's 9-1 co-champion state Class B football team, he was selected 1st team Class B Eastern Conference and 2nd team Class B All-State.

At the University of Arizona, as a 6'3" forward, Edwin captained and was leading scorer on the freshman basketball team. He then led the UofA varsity in scoring and field goal percentage for three years. The 1958 UofA *Desert* (its annual) states, "Ed 'Pudge' Nymeyer set a new University of Arizona record by scoring 1,225 points in three seasons of play." It added, "Nymeyer also broke the 400 mark for the third straight season as he dumped in 408 points." It was later discovered that, with added WWII eligibility years, UofA Hall of Famer Linc Richmond had scored a few points more. Thus, Edwin was instead the UofA's second highest scorer when he graduated. [85]

---

[84] In 2016, B.J. Burries, a Globe High freshman from the San Carlos Reservation east of Globe, scored 68 points in an overtime game. In 2019 the under-sized point guard broke Arizona's all-time career scoring record with 3,387 points in his four-year varsity career. The record was once held by Phoenix Shadow Mountain's Mike Bibby who played for the 1997 NCAA Champion Arizona Wildcats and had a 14-year NBA career. Basketball videos of B.J. can be found on-line.

[85] The authors of "*100 Things Arizona Fans Should Know & Do Before They*

Later, as boys basketball coach of Flowing Wells in Tucson, he led his Caballeros to Arizona's Class A State Championships in 1963 (24-2) and 1968 (24-2). His girls volleyball team also won the Class AAA State Championship in 1992.

In 1997, Edwin was inducted into the University of Arizona Sports Hall of Fame. His plaque reads:

> Outstanding two-sport athlete, finishing his career behind only Linc Richmond in career points scored to date. He was only the third UA player to score 400 points in a season, behind Richmond and Leon Blevins. He broke the school record for free throws made, was second in season scoring average, led his team in scoring three consecutive years and was a three-time All-Border Conference selection. He also lettered in golf one year [Edwin recalls it as two]. He went on to coach at Tucson's Flowing Wells High School, where he became the only coach in Arizona history to record more than 300 wins in two sports: boys' basketball and girls' volleyball. At the time of induction he was the winningest volleyball coach in Arizona high school history and was named the Arizona Daily Star Volleyball Coach of the Year twice (1991 and 1995). He was inducted into the Pima County Sports Hall of Fame in 1995 and the Arizona Coaches Association High School Hall of fame in 1996.

Die" (Anthony Gimino and Steve Rivera) state that, because during World War II wartime competition did not count against eligibility and because freshmen were then allowed to play with the varsity, Linc Richmond was "Arizona's only six year letterman in basketball." They add that in 1946, Richmond's first season back after military service, he scored 21 points in a Madison Square Garden loss to Kentucky. The book also contains a chapter on "Hadie Redd: UA's First African American Player."

In Tucson, Drew McCollough wrote in the Arizona Daily Star:

> **Accomplishments**: Nymeyer led the Wildcats in scoring and field goal percentage for three seasons:
> - **1955-56**: 407 points (15.6 points per game), 42.7 percent
> - **1956-57**: 410 points (15.7 points per game, 51.3 percent
> - **1957-58**: 408 points (15.7 points per game), 43.9 percent
>
> Nymeyer was the captain of the team in 1957-58.

Edwin is a two-sport member of the Arizona High School Athletic Coaches Hall of Fame -- for boys' basketball with 340 wins and two state championships (both at Tucson's Flowing Wells High School); and (also at Flowing Wells HS) for girls' volleyball with 327 wins, nine regional titles, and one state championship.

He was also a charter inductee into Globe High School's Hall of Fame.

In 2003, Edwin's three-man basketball team won the 65-69 division of the Arizona Senior Olympics and finished 12th at the national finals in Virginia. In 2009, at age 73, his three-man team again won the 65-69 division of the Arizona Senior Olympics and finished 9th at the national finals in San Francisco. In 2011, at age 75, his three-man team won the 75 and over division of the Arizona Senior Olympics and finished 3rd at the national finals in Houston (after having lost to the winning team by 1 point and having beaten the runner-up team in the double elimination tourney).

On February 16, 2020 Tucson's Arizona Daily Star sports columnist Greg Hansen published an article headed *"Even at age 83, former Arizona Wildcat Ed Nymeyer can still light it up on basketball court."*

In, 2007, **Lacey Nymeyer**, the grand-daughter of Edwin and his wife Donna, swam on the United States 800-meter freestyle relay swim team that set the world record in the World Games held in Melbourne, Australia. The following year, as a member of the United States 400-meter freestyle relay team, she won a silver medal at the 2008 Beijing Olympics. Although they finished second, they broke the previous Olympic record. In 2009, Lacey was the NCAA Woman Athlete of the year. Extracts from Lacey's University of Arizona's Hall of Fame citation, which termed her "one of the most accomplished student-athletes in Arizona history," read:

> .... A two year co-captain, two-time individual National Champion and eight-time relay National Champion, Lacey's win in the 100 Free at the 2008 National Championship helped Arizona make history and win the first team national title....
>
> The 26-time All-American was named the Pac-10 Women's Swimmer of the Year in 2007.... One of the top swimmers in the country, Lacey also proved to be at the top internationally, as evident by her being on the USA National A-Team for four years and competing in the 2008 Beijing Olympics, where she advanced to the semifinals in the 100 Free and earned a silver medal in the 400 Free Relay while representing Team USA.
>
> A four-time UA Academic Champion, Lacey also excelled in the classroom ... being named ... the 2008 Pac-10 Scholar Athlete of the Year...
>
> ... Lacey was one of only four women in school history to be named the winner of the prestigious NCAA Woman of the Year honor in 2009....

Appendix 9

Selected Writings, Movies and Media Involving Globe-Miami, Gila County and Nearby Superior[86]

Books:

A Little War of Their Own, Don Dedera (Northland Printing Company 1988)

Apache Land, Ross Santee (Scribners, 1947)

Arizona's Dark and Bloody Ground, Earle R. Forrest (University of Arizona Press 1950)

Arizona's Graham-Tewksbury Feud, Leland J. Hanchett, Jr. (Pine Rim Publishing 1994)

The Conquest of Apacheria, Dan L. Thrapp (University of Arizona Press 1967)

Copper Bottom Tales, W.A. Haak (Gila County Historical Society 1991)

Geronimo, Angie Debo (University of Oklahoma Press 1976)

Ghost Riders of the Mogollon, Ivan Lee Kuykendall (Naylor Company 1954)

Globe, Arizona, Clara T. Woody &Milton L. Schwartz (Arizona Historical Society 1977)

---

[86] No effort has been made to make these lists fully inclusive; and they are not. The author regrets that a collection of Globe-Miami essays and anecdotes written by Clarence Duncan, a deceased Jennings Strouss law partner from Globe, was never published. Hopefully, it will be. Clarence was one of what Time-Life Books described in its World War II volume on *China-Burma-India* as the "men of special caliber" – "the swashbuckling pilots of the India-China Wing" who flew supplies over the Himalayas from India into China. It noted, "The Hump took a heavy toll: more than 1,000 men killed and nearly 600 planes lost."

Grover Canyon, Samuel P. Echeveste (2004) (at 2005 Latino Book Awards in New York City, recipient of "Mariposa Award" for Best First Book)

History of Globe Arizona, Donna Anderson (Classic Day Publishing 2007)

The Mighty Miami Vandals, Wilfred "Sonny" Gomez Pena (Hispanic Institute of Social Studies 2008)

Pleasant Valley War, Jinx Pyle (Git A Rope! Publishing, Inc. 2000)

Rose Mofford, First Lady of Arizona, Stephanie McBride-Schreiner

The Summer of 53, Samuel B. Munoz (Hispanic Institute of Social Studies 2005)

To the Last Man (A Story of the Pleasant Valley War), Zane Grey (Harper & Brothers, 1921)[87]

The Truth About Geronimo, Britton Davis (University of Nebraska Press 1929)

Under the Tonto Rim, Zane Grey (Curtis Publishing Company 1925)

We Are Our Memories and Other Writings (Our History, Our Words), Ricardo M. Lucero (Hispanic Institute of Social Studies 2006)

Western Apacheria Raiding and Warfare (University of Arizona Press 1971)

Within Adobe Walls, Helen Baldock Craig (Art-Press Printers 1975)

---

[87] Zane Grey had a cabin near Tonto Creek beneath the Mogollon Rim in northern Gila County where he often wrote. The Northern Gila County Historical Society states that 14 of his books "are set above or below the Mogollon Rim." Two of them are included in this list.

Movies:

The Great White Hope (1970)

White of The Eye (1987)[88]

Midnight Run (1988)[89]

U-Turn (1997) [at Superior 17 miles west of Miami]

Television / Video:

Blood Feuds (2016): The Pleasant Valley War (IMDb) https://www.imdb.com/title/tt5474306 (approx. 44:00)

Forgotten Gunfighters: The Pleasant Valley War https://www.youtube.com/watch?v=hekALWtiWm0 (48:56)

Pleasant Valley War https://www.youtube.com/watch?v=7bwtM2mye6k (29:16)

---

[88] Horror DNA's on-line Blu-ray review describes the protagonist as "an audio-technician living in Globe, Arizona" and the movie as "a beautifully shot psycho-sexual thriller" with cinematography that is "nothing short of stunning."

[89] The movie features scenes in downtown Globe and in steeply rugged Salt River Canyon about 35 miles north where a crash results in a fall off of a cliff into the river. The ensuing rescue involving Robert De Niro and Charles Grodin crashing through river rapids was shot in New Zealand because the Salt River was too cold.

Appendix 10

Arizona Maps

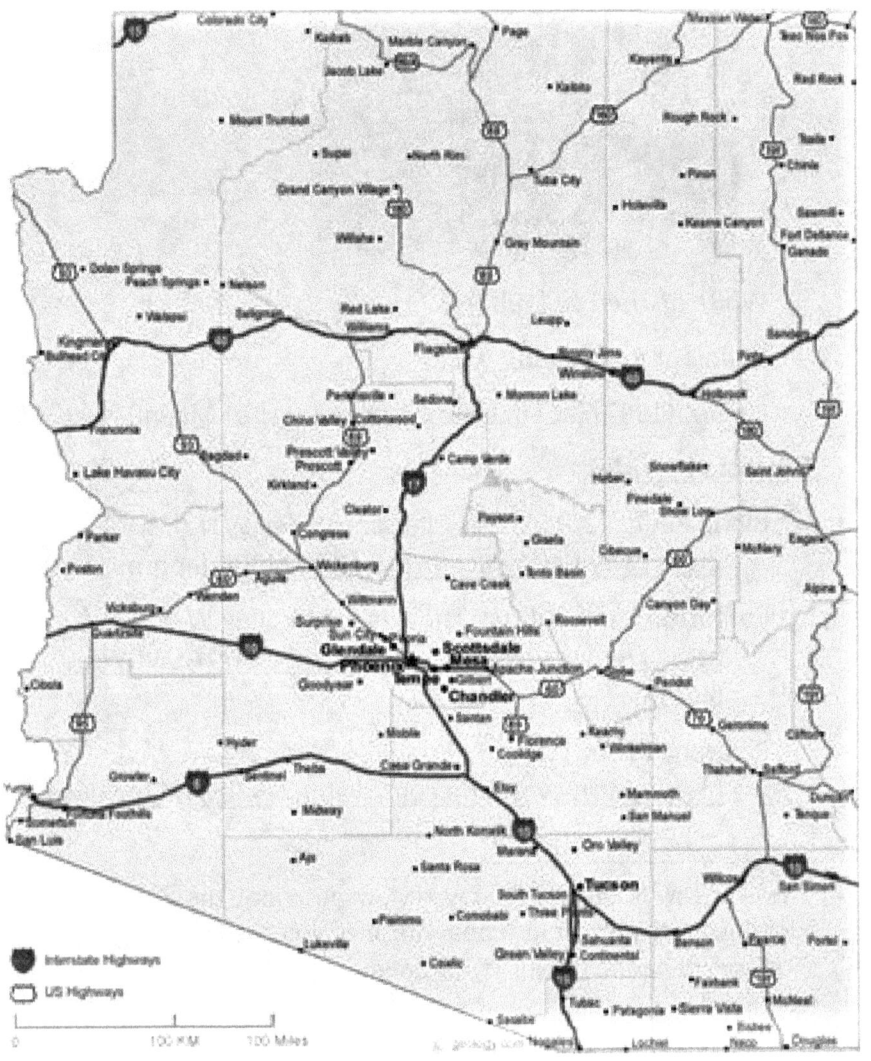

Arizona Interstate and U.S. Highways

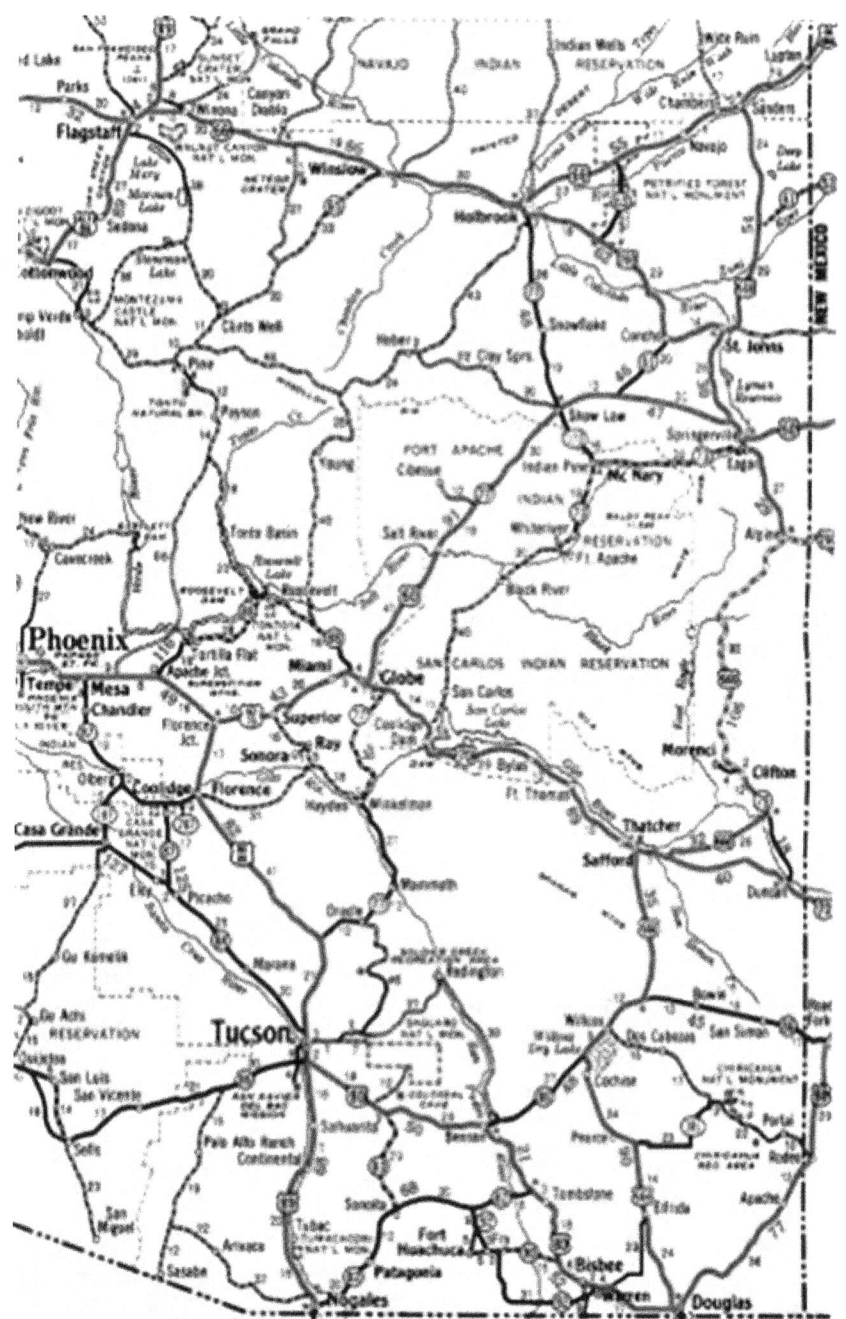

Portion of Arizona with Teams Miami Defeated

About the Author

The author, Gary Keltner, was born in Phoenix, Arizona in 1936. A life-long Arizona resident, he grew up in the East Central Arizona mining and ranching community of Globe. His father (Frank Keltner) managed the J.C. Penney store from 1939 to 1966. His mother ("Hal") was a homemaker who sewed Halloween costumes for Gary and cheerleading outfits for his two sisters and others, enjoyed painting and ceramic artwork, and always welcomed her children's friends into the family home.[90]

Just five years old when the Japanese attacked Pearl Harbor and brought the U.S. into WWII against the Axis powers (Japan, Germany, Italy), the author grew up in a time of national peril and patriotism. "Remember Pearl Harbor" was everywhere. So were images of Uncle Sam pointing at the viewer and exclaiming "We Need You!" Our multi-generational extended family was close and celebrated holidays together, much like those portrayed by Norman Rockwell on Saturday Evening Post magazine covers.

Having grown up during WWII with family members and family friends involved, and then during the Cold War, I and everyone I closely knew in those years was imbued with strongly felt patriotism and related values, believing ours to be the best country and a beacon of hope (as President Reagan later put it, "the shining city on a hill"). I still hold that belief. That so many want to come here and so few choose to leave suggests that I am not alone in that belief.

---

[90] Before zip codes and "modern" communications, telephone calls were made through a switchboard to the Keltner residence (TC# 265) and to the JC Penny Store (TC# 95). The switchboard operators were thought to be privy to too much about the private lives of local families. Many residential numbers were "party lines" that served multiple households. The number of rings would identify the household; and people at other households on the same line could listen in on conversations.

The author is a graduate of Globe High's Class of '54. The Tigers (for whom he played football, basketball and track) were fierce rivals of Miami's Vandals. His senior year football team was state Class B co-champion and beat Miami by a record score. Partisanship was strongly felt and, in those years, player and fan fights during and after Globe-Miami games were not unusual. A night-time football game at Miami ended with players exchanging blows and swinging helmets on the field, as did some Thanksgiving Day games in prior years. He recalls Miami's rabidly anti-Globe administrator (Nick Ragus, a Red Auerbach type) raging in frustration from the announcer's box loudspeaker at a Globe player during the author's last football game (won by Globe at Miami 47-12): "Number 39 [Edward "Chito" Castellanos], cut that out!"[91]

Few were more passionate about the Globe-Miami rivalry than the author. It is ironic that he should be the one to write this chronicle.

Still, even then, the author had friends in Miami and respected their athletes.[92] Privately, he sometimes thought about the athletic powerhouse Globe and Miami would have if, just six miles apart, the schools combined. A union school was considered since, but the

---

[91] "Chito" was a likable, tough, and quietly inspirational teammate. At football practice as an underclassman, he lost front teeth to a forearm, but with replacements had an easy, infectious smile. Playing offensive guard at 139 pounds, at Coolidge he emerged from a pileup with what I recall was a broken collarbone after tackling the Bears' 300-pound fullback. But he stayed on the bench and rode the bus back to Globe that night. The Bears fullback, who later played with Chito at Palo Verde Junior College in Blythe, California, was reportedly out for the season with a broken ankle. Coach Pavlich had told us to hit him low; and Chito did.

[92] Years after having competed against one another, the author met his wife Mary, to whom he has been married since 1967, when Miami's Radovan Vucichevich (known to the author as Lolly) waved him to join a table at which Lolly was sitting with Mary and a friend of hers.

schools never joined.

In high school, the author thought of becoming a sportswriter, but instead became a lawyer -- first with the United States Army's Judge Advocate General's Corps and since 1964 with Jennings Strouss, a Phoenix law firm.

The author graduated from the University of Arizona with degrees in Liberal Arts (1958) and Law (1960), and then spent three years (1961-63) in Army JAGC.

After infantry officer basic training at Ft. Benning, Georgia, and military law school at the University of Virginia in Charlottesville, he was stationed in Washington, D.C. There, he experienced the brink-of-war October 1962 Cuban Missile Crisis, the inspirational August 1963 Martin Luther King March on Washington (during which he was present when Peter, Paul & Mary sang at the Lincoln Memorial), and the somber events of the November 1963 Kennedy assassination.

Before that, while attending the Army's Military Law School on campus at the University of Virginia the author was able to visit Jefferson's Monticello, Monroe's Ash Lawn, Michie Tavern and other nearby and on-campus historic sites. The ill-fated 1961 Bay of Pigs invasion in Cuba occurred while he was in Charlottesville.

During his JAGC years, his interests in history and folk music led him to visit many Civil War sites and to hear live in Charlottesville, D.C. and New York City many of this country's and Canada's most prominent folk singers.

Memorably, the January 1961 bus trip from Globe to Ft. Benning, Georgia, where he was sent for infantry training, exposed the author to eye-opening and disturbing examples of Mississippi and Alabama segregation, including "colored" and "white" entrances on opposite sides at segregated lunch stops and at drive-in theaters, "colored" and "white" drinking fountains, and "men," "women" and "colored" restrooms. In contrast, just across the Alabama state line, in Columbus, Georgia, the author noted none of that; and at Ft. Benning black military instructors were prevalent and among the best.[93]

As a member of Army JAGC's Defense Appellate Division, the author was assigned the only death case to arise during his time there. Joe Livermore, later Dean of the University of Arizona's Law School and an Arizona Court of Appeals Judge, and before that a visiting law professor at Stanford from which he obtained his law degree, was the JAGC Government Appellate Counsel who defended the death sentence.[94]

The accused was a black man who kidnapped and raped two white women (one a teenager) at Fort Dix in New Jersey. The author met with him twice on death row at Fort Leavenworth, Kansas. The author's 1962 appellate brief to an Army Board of Review set forth

---

[93] Adjacent to Columbus, Georgia, Ft. Benning was just across the Chattahoochee River from Phenix City, Alabama. In 1954, a Phenix City lawyer, elected Alabama Attorney General on a platform to reform the city, was shot and killed there. In 1955, *The Phenix City Story* hit the theaters. IMDb describes it as a "semi-documentary" of "an Alabama town ... run by a crime syndicate that's grown fat on prostitution and crooked gambling, directed at soldiers from Fort Benning across the river." Wikipedia states that "Phenix City was notorious during the 1940s and 1950s for being a haven for organized crime, prostitution, and gambling."

[94] Joe and the author became good friends and often during lunch breaks walked the Capital Mall area, including the then accessible underground tunnels connecting federal buildings. Joe was an avid collector of prize-winning Indian blankets and purchased several at the Bureau of Indian affairs while I was with him. Later, when as UofA Law Dean he was in Phoenix to provide an update, he delivered one of the most memorable speeches ever. After a far too long introduction in a too warm room, he stood up and said, "You want to know how things are at the Law School? Well, pretty good." And he sat down.

multiple assignments of error. Two pre-dated later civilian court rulings of broadly applicable significance. One was that the accused's confession was obtained and used without warnings like those the Supreme Court later declared requisite in its landmark 1966 *Miranda* decision, including the rights to remain silent and to counsel.[95] The other was that (in language of the time) "the death sentence is applied unequally to whites and negroes," "particularly when the offense of rape is involved," and that "a man should not ... because he is negro, suffer unequal application of the law." The death sentence was reduced to 30 years. In the context of good conduct and his prior military record, the accused was paroled after 10 years.

Beginning in early 1964, the author is fortunate to have been with Jennings Strouss for almost 60 years. His 15 minutes of fame, continuing to this day, came in 1971 when, selected at random from among others, he officially named the Fiesta Bowl that in 2016 hosted its eighth national championship game.

---

[95] Coincidentally, the *Miranda* case arose out of the kidnapping and rape of a teenager in Phoenix.

www.ingramcontent.com/pod-product-compliance
Lightning Source LLC
Chambersburg PA
CBHW051430290426
44109CB00016B/1498